Critical Thinking across the Curriculum: Building the Analytical Classroom

Victor P. Maiorana
Queensborough Community College

1992

 Clearinghouse on Reading
and Communication Skills

 Press

Published 1992 by:
ERIC Clearinghouse on Reading and Communication Skills
Carl B. Smith, Director
2805 East 10th Street, Suite 150
Bloomington, Indiana 47408-2698
and
EDINFO Press

Editor: Warren Lewis
Cover Design: Lauren Gottlieb
Design: Lauren Gottlieb
Production: Theresa Hardy

ERIC (an acronym for Educational Resources Information Center) is a national network of 16 clearinghouses, each of which is responsible for building the ERIC database by identifying and abstracting various educational resources, including research reports, curriculum guides, conference papers, journal articles, and government reports. The Clearinghouse on Reading and Communication Skills (ERIC/RCS) collects educational information specifically related to reading, English, journalism, speech, and theater at all levels. ERIC/RCS also covers interdisciplinary areas, such as media studies, reading and writing technology, mass communication, language arts, critical thinking, literature, and many aspects of literacy.

This publication was prepared with funding from the Office of Educational Research and Improvement, U.S. Department of Education, under contract no. RI88062001. Contractors undertaking such projects under government sponsorship are encouraged to express freely their judgment in professional and technical matters. Points of view or opinions, however, do not necessarily represent the official view or opinions of the Office of Educational Research and Improvement.

The photo of John Dewey was taken at his summer retreat on Sawlor Lake, Hubbards, Nova Scotia. It was used with permission from Special Collections, Morris Library, Southern Illinois University at Carbondale.

Library of Congress Cataloging-in-Publication Data

Maiorana, Victor P.
    Critical Thinking across the Curriculum : Building the Analytical Classroom / by
    Victor P. Maiorana
        p.   cm.
    ISBN 0-927516-35-7
    1. Critical thinking–Study and teaching–United States.
    2. Educational change–United States.   I. Title.
    LB1590.3.M35 1992   92-20683
    307.15'2–dc20   CIP

ERIC/RCS Advisory Board Members

Joan Baker
Cleveland State University
Cleveland, Ohio

Douglas Barnard
Mesa Public Schools
Mesa, Arizona

Nancy Broz
Language Arts/
Reading Supervisor
Moorestown Public Schools
Moorestown, New Jersy

Jeanne Chall
Reading Center
College of Education
Harvard University
Cambridge, Massachusetts

James Ecke
Dept. of Defense
Dependents' Schools
Centerville, Virginia

George A. Gonzales
Bilingual/Bicultural Program
Pan American University
Edinburg, Texas

Donald Gray
Department of English
Indiana University
Bloomington, Indiana

Richard P. Johns
Dept. of Journalism and
Mass Communication
University of Iowa
Iowa City, Iowa

P. David Pearson
College of Education
University of Illinois
Champaign, Illinois

M. Donald Thomas
Educational Consultant to
Governor of Tennessee
Salt Lake City, Utah

Samuel Weintraub
School of Education
SUNY-Buffalo
Buffalo, New York

Table of Contents

Preface

Consequential solutions to today's educational crisis will not be found in the areas of finance, management, curriculum, school choice, computer technology, television programming, assessment, or testing standards. Solutions lie in providing all classroom teachers with the ability to teach all subject matter to all students in a manner that simultaneously develops students' critical thinking, reading, writing, listening, and speaking skills. These skills mark the thoughtful person, inform the workplace, provide for lifelong learning, and are the human tools of a democracy.

Learning how to teach critical skills and subject matter at the same time, presents to us educators a rare opportunity to reinvent our profession. The purpose of this essay is to offer to you, the classroom teacher, curriculum specialist, educational technologist, or educational administrator, an understanding of how conventional pedagogical practices inhibit the teaching of cognitive skills, and to introduce a thorough, practical, and assessable classroom methodology for teaching cognitive skills throughout the high-school and college curriculum.

Chapter 1 is a discussion of the uses and implications of critical thinking across the curriculum and an introduction of the concept of "the analytical classroom." In chapter 2, I address the purpose of critical thinking, and I provide an overview of the various concepts of critical thinking and their significance for classroom instruction. In chapter 3, I argue that conventional teaching and learning approaches inhibit the development of critical skills in thinking, reading, writing, listening, and speaking. In chapter 4, I present the attributes of my ideal teaching methodology. Chapters 5 through 8 are a thorough introduction to a new thinking/teaching/learning strategy called Means-Ends Critical Analysis of Subject Matter (MECA/SM), a strategy that can be used across the curriculum to teach cognitive skills and subject matter at the same time. In chapter 9, I extend an invitation to apply the MECA/SM analytical approach to a topic in your field of expertise. Chapter 10 is a summary of the principles of the analytical classroom, and it contains a checklist for you to use to determine whether your classroom is an analytical classroom.

I will be happy to comment on any analysis you send me. Send typed analyses to the following address. Please be sure to include your name and address.

Victor P. Maiorana
Room A405
Queensborough Community College
Bayside, New York 11364

I would like to acknowledge the assistance of colleagues and students who have developed many of the analyses that appear herein. A special note of thanks to Warren Lewis, ERIC/RCS Director of Publications, for his encouragement and insightful help in the development and preparation of the manuscript. This book is dedicated to all teachers and students, and especially to Rosalie, Lauren, Joseph, Michael, and Richard.

Victor P. Maiorana
1992

1 What Is Critical Thinking across the Curriculum?

A teaching and learning paradox is undermining American education. Students are expected to develop and demonstrate critical skills while in school and, subsequently, in the workplace. Yet, teachers deliver subject matter in an absolute, crystallized manner that promotes rote memorization rather than critical learning. With the prevailing lecture-for-recall approach to the coursework, little is accomplished in the way of developing those cognitive skills that inform and improve reading, writing, listening, and speaking skills. Indeed, one can make the case that the pervasiveness of the lecture-for-recall method, if not the principal cause, is certainly a major factor in preventing these problems from being solved. The purpose of critical thinking across the curriculum is to change conventional classroom practice so that all teachers will teach critical skills to all students.

The anticipated academic result of critical thinking across the curriculum is the significant improvement of student achievement and retention, and the redesign of teacher-education and faculty-development programs to show teachers how to deliver subject matter while simultaneously teaching critical skills. The anticipated social results of critical thinking across the curriculum are citizens better prepared to live in a democracy, workers better

. . . the pervasiveness of the lecture-for-recall method, if not the principal cause, is certainly a major factor in preventing these problems from being solved.

able to exercise critical energies, and individuals more capable of lifelong learning.

An approach to education that makes every classroom an analytical laboratory provides the basis for addressing several long-standing and vexing challenges faced by American education, including the following: reducing the numbers of high-school and college dropouts, making access meaningful for the underprepared, furthering the prepared, making learning purposeful, and redesigning teacher-education programs.

Empowering the Underprepared

Teachers who use the lecture method (as most teachers do at all levels), subscribe to the content theory of learning and the transmission theory of teaching.

> The knowledgeable (teacher) lectures to the...student so that the student can gain the same knowledge. Such an approach clearly favors highly motivated students and those who tend to be avid readers and good listeners. Students who read slowly or who have no intrinsic interest in the subject matter of a particular course are not well served by this approach. (Astin, 1985)

According to content transmission theory, students are empty vessels that must be filled up with memorized knowledge; moreover, students are thought to be unable to think critically in a given subject-matter area until its basic facts and ideas have been transmitted to them.

Because teachers rely on content transmission theory, students remain poorly prepared not only for the task of learning itself but also for the contemporary workplace. The lecture method wrings subject matter dry of its inherent interest and dynamics, and it induces boredom. Students cite boredom as the major cause of their dropping interest, their dropping of motivation, and their dropping-out. (Astin, 1975)

Lecture-for-recall goes beyond being merely boring. It imposes large academic penalties both on the prepared student and on the learning-disadvantaged and those with limited English proficiency. These penalties include the following:

- Topics are presented sequentially, not critically, thus depriving both student and teacher of a dynamic understanding of the subject matter.

- Students are not critically engaged; therefore, they remain passive and accepting.

- Because critical connections within the subject matter are not made for them, and since they are not shown how to make these connections for themselves, students come to an entirely logical conclusion: They had better memorize the material. Memorization of material causes them to place a premium on rote-learning skills, including note-taking in class, textbook underlining, and cramming, skills which many students from insufficiently literate backgrounds lack.

- Because students are placed in a passive role, they have little hope of individualized in-class help from the teacher. The teacher does most of the talking, questioning, and thinking; hence the teacher—not the students—gets most of the practice in using the English language and using communicative and academic skills. The teacher learns a lot; the students are bored.

The lecture method, further, is also a significant factor in denying intellectual access to special populations with literacy problems. The skills required by rote learning are exactly the skills those with limited English proficiency, the disadvantaged, and the underprepared lack. They therefore do not respond well to the classroom lecture method and rote learning. There is evidence that

The lecture method, further, is also a significant factor in denying intellectual access to special populations with literacy problems.

African-American and other ethnic-minority students are disproportionately affected by these learning penalties. According to Nelson-Barber and Meir (1990), Black students underachieve because they see the classroom as serving no practical purpose. Although students may gain physical access to schools, colleges, and universities, this physical access is not meaningful to them because the teaching methodologies that they encounter block their intellectual access.

Yet another penalty associated with content transmission theory is that students themselves cannot gauge what they are learning; they have no way of knowing when their state of learning requires improvement. Their learning must be validated by their teacher, not by themselves. The only way they can assess their learning is through scores made on objective tests which generally test recall. "[If] the only function of learners is to reproduce precisely what is out there, [then] this is a model for frustrated teachers, bored students, cramming for exams, objective test items, high drop-out rates, and alienation." (Shermis, 1992) Unless the problem of classroom methodology is addressed in an aggressive manner, "Attempts to expand educational opportunities for underprepared students [will] probably [be] hindered by continued reliance of most faculty members on the content theory of learning." (Astin, 1985)

In sum, students are not asked to do the one thing that they are capable of, the one thing that they did very well at age five, but which their subsequent education has schooled out of them: They are not asked to think for themselves and to question. Does it not make sense to suggest that if teachers were to build methodologically on an innate skill already possessed by students, a skill which they are eager to apply and which can be nurtured, that students would persist and achieve at higher and higher levels? This is the essence of what critical thinking across the curriculum is about. This is the promise of the impact it can have.

For the most part, teachers deliver, and students receive, crystalized intelligence. Each course may be thought of as an individual crystal, a stated body of presumably absolute knowledge delivered in an authoritarian manner meant to promote unquestioning acceptance on the part of the student. The task of the prepared student (that is, a student who can learn by rote) is to gain possession of the crystals in a given content area in order to pass the course. Going from class to class, students gather a handful of crystals which they ultimately present as a justification for going to the next grade or level. When enough crystals are gathered, even though they may be dropped as soon as they are no longer needed, graduation ensues.

The trouble with crystallized intelligence is that it serves primarily one purpose only: to pass the course. Gathering a crystal requires no independent and analytical thought. The best way for students to gather crystals is to make their version of facts and truths conform exactly to that held by the teacher. Because they are asked primarily to memorize, not to analyze, students see no intellectual relationship within or among the crystals, no way of merging them into a comprehensive kaleidoscope of subject matter. Indeed, the very idea of merging crystals is antithetical to the authoritative absolutism that crystallized intelligence represents. Furthermore, the delivered crystal, however cloudy and chipped, is often the same crystal that the teacher dispensed last semester, and it is probably the same crystal that the teacher received from his or her own teacher. So the cycle continues, down through the ages, over hundreds and hundreds of years, until one day we look up to discover that really nothing in the way of teaching and learning has changed in the last 2,500 years. The comparisons that follow show how rigid is the practice

Challenging the Crystal Gatherers

of teaching and learning when compared to other areas of human endeavor in which cognitive processes have guided and developed methodology:

The Evolution of Key Areas
versus
The Frozen State of Teaching and Learning

Transportation:	walking, horse and buggy, railroad, automobile, airplane, spacecraft
Communication:	telegraph, telephone, radio, television, computers
Illumination:	firelight, candlelight, gaslight, electric light
Calculation:	fingers, pebbles, abacus, mechanical adding machine, electronic computer
Engineering:	trial-and-error, rule-of-thumb, scientific formulations
Law:	archaic (mystical), primitive (oral), civilized (written)
Medicine:	incantation, blood-letting, modern surgery
Teaching:	lecture method, *no evolution*
Learning:	rote learning, *no evolution*
Textbooks:	sequential, non-critical, discussion of subject matter; *no evolution*

From the time about 2,500 years ago in Sicily when Corax started to teach oratory, to the present day, remarkably little has changed in the classroom. Like a crystal, teaching and learning is frozen in time.

What is wrong with crystal gathering? Nothing in and of itself, but don't expect the crystals to fit together in a systematic way; don't expect crystal gathering to result in an understanding of how various parts of a system fit together; don't expect crystals to provide a basis for developing cognitive skills; and don't expect a crystal from one area to inform, or bear a relationship to, another area. Furthermore, don't be surprised when you learn that crystalized knowledge is failing to inform the fast-paced workplace, our culture of lifelong learning, or society in which independent, fluid, resilient, and analytical thought is a key ingredient to the survival of our democracy.

One way or another, prepared students have learned how to collect crystals. Because they possess rote-learning skills, prepared students can do very well in a lecture-for-recall environment. Their cognitive skills, nevertheless, are not developed, and they remain more or less cognitively frozen at essentially the fourth-grade, recall level. In effect, their development as thoughtful, independent thinkers is ill-served. Trapped in the ice crystals of an intellectual iceberg, they are constrained to learn every subject by rote; they hold their crystals until the time when tests are over so that they, with grateful relief, can let this semester's collection of crystals melt and run through their fingers because it has finished serving its rote-learning purpose.

Critical thinking across the curriculum is aimed at dashing all the crystals and melting the iceberg. Its purpose is to change a situation in which the underprepared student drops out, and the prepared student receives crystallized intelligence only. Its effect will be to introduce all students to the dynamic elements that comprise subject matter, and bring all students—through analysis, evaluation, inquiry, and problem-solving—to build a critical understanding of subject matter. Theirs will not be the quiet knowledge of the teacher and the textbook. Theirs will be a dynamic appreciation of knowledge and its mutability—a realization that subject matter is not inviolate, that it can change, and that those who have learned how to deal with the dynamics of subject matter—having learned how to learn—will be able to survive in an increasingly complex world.

Critical thinking across the curriculum is aimed at dashing all the crystals and melting the iceberg. Its purpose is to change a situation in which the underprepared student drops out, and the prepared student receives crystallized intelligence only. Its effect will be to introduce all students to the dynamic elements that comprise subject matter, and bring all students—through analysis, evaluation, inquiry, and problem-solving—to build a critical understanding of subject matter.

Making Learning Purposeful

Babies, children, and adults are by nature purposeful and goal-directed. Their purposes may be lofty or hollow, agreeable or aggravating, but they are nonetheless purposeful. Purpose is a life force. The typical content-theory approach to classroom teaching, however, is a stark contradiction to natural purposiveness. Teachers and students are accustomed to seeing teaching and learning in terms of classroom lectures and textbook presentations. The belief is that knowing subject matter is all about learning objectives, class notes, and topic headings; the sequential presentation of topics in the lecture and the textbook is a sterile, non-critical, and misguided view of subject matter. At all academic levels and in all subjects, the emphasis is on rote learning. Students are told, or it is implied, that what they receive in the classroom may, in some unspecified way, be of use to them in the future.

With this approach, we remove purpose from the classroom and from the subject matter; we blunt students' instinct for the relevant. Students are not shown how to transform or reconstruct subject matter; hence they themselves are not transformed into critical analysts, readers, writers, and speakers. Seeing no purpose to the classroom or the subject matter at hand, students quite logically learn to rely on their memory, rather than on their inventiveness. Students are not able to assess their own learning achievements because the traditional classroom has taught them to be passive learners. They find it hard to engage in life-long learning because they have been taught *what* to learn, not *how* to learn. They have minimal basic and critical skills on which to build a future in the workplace. In this manner, they are denied access to higher levels of education, workplace opportunities, and the skills necessary for life-long learning. Students learn by rote because the teacher's teaching method becomes the students' learning message.

Critical thinking across the curriculum is aimed at changing classrooms from rigid intelligence that is rote learning to dynamic intelligence that is analytical learning.

A key concept of critical thinking across the curriculum is that any and all subject matter can provide the basis for developing cognitive skills in students. "It is desirable to expel...the...notion that some subjects are inherently 'intellectual,' and hence possessed of an almost magical power to train the faculty of thought.... Any subject from Greek to cooking...is intellectual...in its power to start and direct significant inquiry and reflection." (Dewey, 1933) The case for the cognitive equality of subject matter must constantly be made. Oft-repeated sentiments make clear the continuing belief that certain subjects are better suited than others to teaching thinking skills.

"The only way to teach history critically is to teach your students to think like a historian."

"To learn mathematics properly one must learn to think like a mathematician."

"To study chemistry critically, one must learn to think like a scientist."

Because it is manifestly not possible to teach students to become experts within the confines of time, class size, and expected content coverage, these sentiments are self-defeating. They place insurmountable burdens on teachers. Faced with the undoable, many teachers throw up their hands and retire to the quiet comfort of the lecture method.

Even when we state our approval of critical thinking, we seem to be constructing an intellectual tower of cognitive incoherence in which each discipline must have its own crystallized approach to teaching critical thinking. These approaches encourage isolation, and they fractionalize the education profession, driving members of the profession apart in diverse quests to have teachers plant critical skills in students, as though the urge to ask questions were not innate in every human mind.

Reinventing Teacher Education and Faculty Development

*Critical thinking
across the curri-
culum provides
the framework
for improving
teacher perfor-
mance as re-
gards the
development of
cognitive skills
in students. It al-
lows us to re-
think what is
done in the class-
room, and to
what ends
classwork should
be devoted. Most
of all, it is aimed
at transforming
students intellec-
tually, at rescu-
ing them from
being passive in
the acceptance
of subject matter
and making
them active ana-
lyst of subject
matter.*

"[M]athematical processes...are natural and inherent in all of us. It seems to me that mathematics education is about helping people to release those powers and to apply them in certain contexts; to awaken or release the inner pattern seeker." (Mason, 1991) The same may be said of critical thinking: It is natural and inherent in all of us. Everyone in every discipline, teachers and students alike, all are critical thinkers in the sense that they possess the ability to question, inquire, and discover. This ability is not tied to the study of any one subject matter; all subject matters can be used as a basis for developing, demonstrating, and assessing cognitive skills. Critical thinking is an innate ability, always present, but it needs to be recognized, drawn out, made manifest. The rote-inducing content-theory approach to education has the effect of undermining the teaching of cognitive skills. Teacher educators need to ask themselves how they can prepare all teachers to develop, and not undermine, critical thinking skills. All teachers, across all grades and curricula, need to exhibit and demonstrate critical thinking skills. In this way, a profession will be developed that more directly serves teachers, students, and society.

Do teachers have a responsibility to develop critical thinking? "It would certainly seem so because every school curriculum lists critical thinking and critical reading as a major performance objective." (Smith, 1990) Critical thinking across the curriculum provides the framework for improving teacher performance as regards the development of cognitive skills in students. It allows us to rethink what is done in the classroom, and to what ends classwork should be devoted. Most of all, it is aimed at transforming students intellectually, at rescuing them from being passive in the acceptance of subject matter and making them active analysts of subject matter. By showing teachers that they can do more than merely transmit subject matter, they will come to appreciate the new intelligence that will guide their practice. Because of the potential impact of critical analysis on improved student performance, administrators; curriculum designers; and state, local, and federal policy makers must see their primary responsibility as assisting classroom teachers in their quest to help students become independent thinkers and life-long learners. Critical thinking across the curriculum is the primary means of achieving this end.

The problems of low academic achievement, high drop-out rates, and the lack of critical skills in the workplace will not be solved by administrators concerned with efficiency and assessment, school boards preoccupied with finances and local control, or state-sponsored curriculum designers concerned with content coverage and testing. These problems are unlikely to be solved by federal programs that seek to impose uniformity of results through a national exam, thus assuring that the lecture-for-recall method will survive for yet another 2,500 years! These problems will be solved primarily by classroom teachers employing methodologies that transform their students' cognitive processes.

Stated another way, the major challenge of American education is not financial, curricular, or managerial; rather, it is a methodological challenge: How can we change teachers and students, at all levels and in all disciplines, from being passive acceptors/memorizers of subject matter to being active, critical analysts and evaluators of subject matter? This is the essence of what is meant by critical thinking across the curriculum: Teachers showing students, regardless of the discipline, how to engage in learning not only as an act of memory but also as an act of analysis and evaluation. How to accomplish this change is the special purpose of this essay.

. . .the major challenge of American education is not financial, curricular, or managerial; rather, it is a methodological challenge: How can we change teachers and students, at all levels and in all disciplines, from being passive acceptors/memorizers of subject matter to being active, critical analysts and evaluators of subject matter?

2 What Is the Purpose of Critical Thinking?

We engage in critical thinking whenever we face a situation like the following:

- When presented with a situation that we do not understand, our intellectual instinct is to try to make some sense of it. This attempt to make sense starts with the child's asking "Why?" It continues throughout life.

- When presented with a viewpoint or position with which we do not agree, or that we have cause to doubt, we (ideally) seek to discover the basis for the suspect viewpoint. If we satisfactorily explore the viewpoint, we can then either accept or reject it based upon our discoveries.

- When presented with a problem, we will (usually) take the steps necessary to effect a solution.

The purpose of critical thinking is, therefore, to achieve understanding, evaluate viewpoints, and solve problems. Since all three areas involve the asking of questions, we can say that critical thinking is the questioning or inquiry we engage in when we seek to understand, evaluate, or resolve.

Various Views of Critical Thinking

"Critical thinking" has been defined in different ways. An understanding of these varying interpretations will inform your teaching and practice of critical thinking, your lesson-plan designs, and your selection of associated materials. Descriptions of critical thinking fall into three broad categories: definitional, taxonomic, and procedural.

Definitional Representations of Critical Thinking

Brookfield (1987) described critical thinking as questioning the assumptions that underlie our habitual ways of thinking. Black (1952) discussed critical thinking as either inductive or deductive thinking. For Bruner (1966), it was the ability to form hypotheses. For McPeck, it was the ability to reflect and seek truth in a given area of knowledge. (Smith, 1990) For Meyers (1986), it was the ability to produce generalizations, see new possibilities, and defer judgment. For Paul (1990), it was reflective digestion. For Shermis (1992), it was reflective inquiry. For Smith (1990), it included analyzing, drawing inferences, and making judgements on the basis of some standards. For Taba (1959), it was generalizing, concluding, or comparing and contrasting. For Werthheimer (1964), it was productive thinking that leads to advances in knowledge.

Taxonomic Descriptions of Critical Thinking

Cognitive Taxonomy

Bloom, Engelhart, Furst, Hill, and Krathwohl (1956) classified educational goals in their *Taxonomy of Educational Objectives—Cognitive Domain*. The "Bloom taxonomy" concerns knowledge recall and development of intellectual skills and abilities. The taxonomy is an organization of cognitive processes falling within a hierarchy of categories beginning with knowledge and proceeding up through the levels of comprehension, application, analysis, synthesis, and evaluation. Bloom *et al.* described the categories as linear and cumulative. For example, to think at the analysis level, one must pass sequentially through, and operate at, the levels of knowledge, comprehension, and application. The sequence itself, and the idea that thinking is sequential in the manner of the taxonomy, is open to question. For example, some researchers placed "synthesis" between "knowledge" and "comprehension." (Seddon, 1978, p. 310) In 1980, I argued that synthesis (in the sense of creative thought) belongs above evaluation, and I still think so. (Maiorana, 1980, p. 240) Although the Bloom taxonomy does not address teaching for critical thinking, it provides a basis for formulating instructional models aimed at developing critical-thinking skills.

Developmental Hierarchy

Piaget (1977) believed that his hierarchy of thinking stages was biologically (developmentally) based, paralleling a child's mental development.

- *Sensory-motor*: use of verbal symbols

- *Preoperational*: irreversible thinking based on perception

- *Concrete operations*: analyzing, classifying

- *Formal operations*: imaginative, conceptual thinking

Learned Capabilities and Intellectual Skills

Gagne (1974) developed categories for human capabilities to aid in the development of instructional systems. The categories are intellectual skills, cognitive strategies, verbal information, motor skills, and attitudes. Perceived not as a linear hierarchy, these categories were thought to be parallel.

Critical Thinking Strategies

Paul (1990) described three categories of critical thinking: affective strategies, cognitive strategies (macro-abilities), and cognitive strategies (micro-skills). Affective strategies include thinking independently; becoming sensitive to egocentricity and sociocentricity; suspending judgment; being fair-minded; exploring underlying thoughts and feelings; and developing intellectual confidence, humility, courage, integrity, and perseverance.

Cognitive strategies (macro-abilities) include clarifying words, phrases, texts, issues, conclusions, and beliefs; analyzing, comparing, exploring, creating, and evaluating arguments, interpretations, theories, actions, solutions, and policies; making interdisciplinary connections; reasoning dialogically and dialectically through Socratic questioning, transferring insights to new contexts.

Cognitive strategies (micro-skills) include using critical vocabulary, noting similarities and differences, comparing and contrasting, identifying assumptions and evaluating, distinguishing the important from the trivial, seeing contradictions, exploring implications and consequences, evaluating evidence and alleged facts, and making plausible interpretations.

Other Taxonomies

Ennis described twelve critical-thinking skills, including understanding the meaning of a statement, judging ambiguity, judging whether an inductive conclusion is warranted, and judging whether statements made by authorities are acceptable. (Smith, 1990) Guilford's (1977) intellectual structures include five cognitive operations: cognition, memory, divergent production, convergent production, and evaluation. The last three of these could be classified as critical-thinking oriented. Thomas' (1972) higher-order cognitive taxonomy includes the categories of learning-to-learn skills, communications skills, classifying and comparing skills, synthesizing and producing skills, judging and inferring skills, and skills of valuing and decision-making. Seif (1981) categorized future-thinking skills (critical-thinking and problem-solving skills needed for the future) according to six patterns: scientific, creative, anticipating, complex systems, mutual needs, and ethical values.

Procedural or Process-oriented Descriptions of Critical Thinking

Problem-solving Process

The procedural steps involved in the problem-solving process as described by 20th-century educators stem from the reflective thought of John Dewey and his description of the process. According to Dewey in *How We Think* (originally published in 1910, restated in 1933), the five phases of the reflective thought process are these:

1. *Suggestions*, in which the mind leaps forward to a possible solution

2. An intellectualization of the difficulty or perplexity that has been felt (directly experienced) into a *problem* to be solved, a question for which an answer must be sought

3. The use of one suggestion after another as a leading idea, or **hypothesis**, to initiate and guide observation and other operations in collection of factual material

4. The mental **elaboration** of the idea or supposition as cognitive construct (*reasoning*, in the sense in which reasoning is a part, not the whole, of inference)

5. **Testing** the hypothesis by overt or imaginative action (p. 107)

The influence of Dewey's reflective-thought process is widely recognized. "Dewey single-handedly gave one of the best descriptions ever written on the logic of solving a problem." (Rugg, 1952, p. 269) Following Dewey,

Dewey Challenges the Crystal Gatherers

Greenfield (1987), Woods (1987), and Whimby and Whimbey (1975) described critical thinking as a patterned or habitual approach to problem-solving. Stoner (1982) described a decision-making process that parallels Dewey's phases:

- diagnose and define the problem

- gather and analyze relevant facts

- develop solutions

- evaluate the solutions, decide on the best solution

- analyze the possible consequences of the decision carry out the decision

A variant of this procedure is called "systems analysis" (Semprevivo, 1976), and an approach that addresses creative thinking is Osborn's creative problem-solving process:

- fact-finding

- idea-finding

- solution-finding

Parnes (1977) offered a variation on this approach.

Syllogistic Analysis

A syllogism follows logical analysis as in "if-then" reasoning. The aim of syllogistic thought is to determine whether a series of statements is logically related and deductively correct.

Critical Analysis

Socrates is still our great teacher of analysis through questioning of statements, ideas, or positions in order to reveal hidden assumptions, implied premises, and inappropriate inferences. The aim of critical analysis is to determine the underlying validity associated with a speaker's or writer's thoughts or ideas.

Means-Ends Critical Analysis of Subject Matter (MECA/SM)

I propose a method of arranging subject matter so as to show its purpose or meaning. This approach involves identifying, categorizing, and relating the means and ends that are present in all subject matter so that purposes can be revealed and consequences evaluated. MECA/SM analysis typically begins by determining an end-in-view (purpose), identifying and arranging the means necessary to achieve the end-in-view, and then considering the likely consequences of achieving the end-in-view. (Maiorana, 1980, 1984, 1992) The discussion of MECA/SM in this book begins with Chapter 5.

The question: "What do you mean when you say 'critical thinking'?" is appropriately asked when discussing critical thinking across the curriculum. Considering the variety of views on critical thinking, a discussion of critical thinking with teachers, students, parents, authors, curriculum designers, and administrators, needs to begin with an understanding of what the other person has in mind with the phrase "critical thinking" and the contexts in which critical thought will be exercised.

For example, people who think of critical thinking merely in terms of making definitions, are not likely to perceive that critical thinking can have something to do with subject matter in a course. Many people tend to believe that critical thinking is something good, but that it is not something that can be taught; they are unaware that taxonomies, although they are not teaching methodologies, may be used to cast subject matter in a critical-thinking perspective. An example of this is the instructional approach called "expansion questioning" in which teachers develop classroom questions that parallel

Significance of Various Views on Critical Thinking

The more flexible and accepting we are of the many dimensions of critical thinking, and the many ways that critical thinking can be taught, the more we distance ourselves from the cold and cognitively unrewarding climate of crystallized intelligence.

Bloom's cognitive levels. If a procedural or problem-solving view of critical thinking is taken, one may (mistakenly) conclude that these procedures can be used only after students gain familiarity with the subject matter through use of the conventional lecture-for-recall method.

When considering the adoption of classroom materials, it is important to ask upon which conceptual foundation the instructional materials are designed. You must ask the question if you are to understand the potential impact of the materials on the development of cognitive skills. In many instructional programs in critical thinking, the teaching of critical skills is isolated from classroom subject matter itself. These programs send the wrong signals to teachers and students alike, namely, that critical thinking has little or nothing to do with the real subject matter of school work; that what one teaches and studies in class is not, and cannot be, related to critical thinking.

The availability of many perspectives on critical thinking also serves an important pedagogical purpose. The many perspectives provide a basis for the development of corresponding teaching methodologies, with the chance that one or more of the methodologies, by itself or in concert with others, may prove useful in the classroom.

Educators are less successful when they try to force a uniform interpretation of critical thinking. The more flexible and accepting we are of the many dimensions of critical thinking, and the many ways that critical thinking can be taught, the more we distance ourselves from the cold and cognitively unrewarding climate of crystallized intelligence.

3 Why We Normally Fail to Teach Critical Thinking in the Classroom

Barriers to Teaching Critical Thinking

S.D. Brookfield stated that teaching critical thinking in the classroom is "an abstract academic pastime" and that real-life critical-thinking skills are a "lived activity" better taught to adults. (Brookfield, 1987, p. 15) While Brookfield believed that the academic setting for critical thinking is crucial, he also affirmed that these activities are most difficult to achieve in the classroom. He devoted almost all of his book to adults in a non-classroom setting. "This book takes the concepts of critical thinking, analysis, and reflection out of the classroom and places them firmly in the context of adults' lives—in their relationships, at their workplaces, in their political involvements, and in their reactions to mass media of communication." (p. 12) Although Brookfield essentially ignored the high-school and university curriculum, his chapter on "Effective Strategies for Fostering Critical Thinking" is helpful regarding the type of atmosphere necessary in a classroom environment that supports critical thinking. M.C. Hoeke (1989) similarly reasoned that analysis and evaluation of subject matter are not possible because it is difficult to analyze these levels of achievement, especially in the use of microcomputer software.

Although the views that the classroom is not appropriate for teaching "real" critical-thinking skills, and that the evaluation of those skills is difficult, are not wide-spread in the literature, I believe that they are widespread in the profession. Because English and philosophy departments have traditionally taught thinking skills, teachers in other departments have not generally perceived critical thinking as part of their teaching job. Furthermore, teaching students to think critically seems difficult; therefore, most teachers hesitate to undertake it.

Is the classroom too artificial a forum for teaching practical, real-life thinking skills?

Is the classroom too artificial a forum for teaching practical, real-life thinking skills? Must the job be left to the traditional experts? Can we teachers, regardless of our subject-matter area, teach critical-thinking skills in the high-school and college classroom? Despite the swelling tide of research, writing, and symposia on the topic, the answer is by no means clear. At least five reasons, all associated with conventional pedagogical practice, cause us to hesitate as teachers of critical-thinking skills: We confuse methodology with organization, we rely too much on textbooks, we underestimate subject matter, we teach *about* the subject matter rather than teaching the subject matter *itself*, and we have limited awareness of what it means to teach critical-thinking skills.

We Confuse Classroom Organization with Methodology

In order properly to evaluate teaching schemes, it is important to distinguish between teaching methodology and teaching organization. A teaching methodology is about how the *subject matter* is arranged and presented. Teaching organization is about how the *participants* in the learning situation are arranged. Making this distinction allows us to determine whether the idea being proffered actually addresses the teaching of subject matter or is merely another form of classroom organization.

For example, if a teacher uses Bloom's cognitive taxonomy as a basis for asking questions about the subject matter at hand (an approach referred to as "expansion questioning"), then that is a teaching methodology. If, however, a teacher places students in groups, and asks them to discuss a topic together, then that is a form of teaching organization. In other words, methodology is based on some subject-matter framework or theory; organization is based on arranging students to study the subject matter. On this basis, student panels, learning contracts, portfolios, role-playing, and field trips are organizational forms. These approaches are useful for critical thinking only to the extent that they cause students to transform or reconstruct the given subject matter.

We Rely Too Much on Textbooks

Textbooks are statements of generally accepted knowledge. Rarely do textbook authors attempt to challenge accepted conventions. They present crystallized, ready-made subject matter, which is expected to be learned as presented. With few exceptions, texts in a given subject-matter area all bear a striking resemblance in terms of their topics and manner of presentation. Textbooks are ultimately authoritarian in that they represent a one-way communication with no possibility for the reader (teacher or student) to ask questions. To paraphrase Paulo Freire (1989, p. 35), textbooks produce answers without any questions having been asked.

Textbooks present many other serious problems with profound implications for how teachers are educated and students are taught. Not only do textbooks have a pervasive influence on *what* is taught in the classroom but also they dictate *how* subject matter is to be taught. Based on what is printed, the most we can expect from authors is logical thinking, not critical thinking. You can see this for yourself by looking at the table of contents in standard texts for any area in the high-school or college curriculum, especially those texts in the career areas. The material is presented in neat subdivisions within major topics. The presentation is sequential, not critical. You will rarely see

Textbooks are ultimately authoritarian in that they represent a one-way communication with no possibility for the reader (teacher or student) to ask questions.

topics arranged to show their purposes, underlying assumptions analyzed, or associated problem-solving techniques presented. As classroom teachers, we compound the *authors' sterile presentation* by adopting the textbook's sequential presentations as *our own teaching methodology*. Thereby we miss the chance to arrange subject matter to show its purpose, challenge assumptions, and discuss problem-solving. The consequence is a lecture format that induces rote learning.

We Underestimate Subject Matter

Rather than dealing with the dynamics of subject matter, many educators go to great lengths to disguise it. We do this by emphasizing glossy four-color textbooks, photography, and beautiful illustrations, and—ironically—student study guides. We separate knowledge from the purposes it serves. We disassociate subject matter from its meaning by emphasizing surface understandings. We muffle, we stifle, we strangle subject matter's inherent excitement.

Subject matter is any material that is capable of inquiry. It represents accumulated wisdom to date, but it is by no means inviolate. Subject matter is subject to change as new ideas, discoveries, and practices reshape, alter, and update it. Merely reading about subject matter, or studying it in order to memorize it, does not reveal its true nature. Course content as it appears in textbooks and other forms of educational technology, is merely raw material. It must be intelligently processed in some fashion if students are to gain understanding. Raw subject matter has only potential value, and it is not inherently intellectual.

By critical-thinking standards, no one subject matter is better than another for fostering critical-thinking skills. The material in any text is raw until it has been processed in some fashion by the individual. It is the processing of subject matter that can eventually lead to true mastery of that subject matter. The nature of the processing determines at what level the subject matter will be mastered. If one merely reads the raw subject matter, only a surface familiarity will be gained. If one sets out to study the raw subject matter by memorizing certain aspects, then a recall ability will be gained. Only if the subject matter is processed in a manner that requires the individual to analyze it critically, will a meaningful understanding be gained.

All subject matter is alive with meaning. It pursues some purpose, and it teems with processes that achieve its purpose. It uses persons, places, and things in support of its purposes. Subject matter has consequences that can be revealed once we have identified its purposes. All of these elements have a dynamic relationship, and there are no absolute starting and ending points. The elements of subject matter become meaningful only when we place them in a context that reveals their purposeful relationships. Because we underestimate subject matter, we rob it of these dynamic attributes; we deny the joy of learning that accompanies their discovery. These dynamic attributes exist even in the driest textbook presentation. I believe that the underestimation ("subject matter is dull") and misconception ("subject matter is something to be memorized") of subject matter are what accounts for the almost exclusive reliance on the mind-as-vessel philosophy and drill-and-practice teaching and learning going on in our schools.

It is up to us as teachers to discover for ourselves, and then help our students to discover, the inherent dynamism that is at the center of all subject matter. We must shape raw subject matter into a form that will allow the individual to appreciate the true nature of the subject matter. The discovery of these relationships is at once both the reason for, and the reward of, education. Pointing to these relationships is the special work of the teacher.

The elements of subject matter become meaningful only when we place them in a context that reveals their purposeful relationships. Because we underestimate subject matter, we rob it of these dynamic attributes; we deny the joy of learning that accompanies their discovery. These dynamic attributes exist even in the driest textbook presentation.

The one major step we must take if we are to reveal the inherent dynamics of subject matter is to appreciate the difference between teaching that is *about* the subject matter and teaching what is *within* the subject matter itself.

We Teach <u>about</u> the Subject Matter, not the Subject Matter <u>Itself</u>

Textbook material (and other forms of subject-matter delivery such as TV, audio tapes and disks, films, and computer courseware) can be analyzed from at least two major standpoints: 1) What is the author's purpose in discussing the subject matter? 2) What is the purpose of the subject matter itself? Both of these purposes are present in, and can be drawn from, the same textual material. If one is going to teach for critical thinking, it is important to distinguish between the author's purpose and the subject matter's own purpose.

One way of drawing the distinction is to recognize that an author's purpose in discussing subject matter is generally summarized as a stated series of objectives. These objectives, which are meant to represent the product of teaching and learning, are *about* the subject matter; they are not drawn from *within* the subject matter itself. The purposes to which one can put subject matter are the ends that subject matter serves; these purposes are what gives meaning to subject matter. These ends are inherent *within* the subject matter, they are not *about* the subject matter. Let's look at some examples:

Typically an author's purpose (in this case, a math teacher's purpose) is stated as an objective:

- *The student shall understand fractions.*

The subject matter's purpose—in this case, the purpose of a fraction—is not the same as the teacher's purpose:

- The purpose of a fraction is to represent a numeric value that is less than one.

The first statement is *about* the subject matter. The second arises from *within* the subject matter itself.

In another example, the first statement is *about* the subject matter; the second statement comes from *within* the subject matter itself.

Here is the computer teacher's purpose, but not the subject matter's purpose:

- *The students shall be able to describe the advantages of a computer.*

Here is the computer's (that is, the subject matter's) purpose:

- *The purpose of a computer is to increase the user's capacity to do intelligent work and to be productive.*

A third example to make clear the distinction between a statement that is *about* the subject matter, and a statement that comes from *within* the subject matter itself, comes from physiology:

Here is the teacher's purpose, but not the subject matter's purpose:

- *The student shall understand the digestive system.*

Here is the digestive system's purpose, but not the teacher's purpose:

- The digestive system extracts nutrients from food.

These examples show that we teachers confuse process with product. Our preoccupation with product-based learning objectives causes us to lose cite of the purposes and processes inherent in all subject matter. We are outside the store looking in through the display window. We never enter the store to look around and appraise and select; we don't make the purchase, so the subject matter is not ours to keep. The subject may be remembered, but it is never grasped. The unintended consequence, however well-meaning we be, is that we foster rote learning at the sacrifice of developing critical thinking. Second only to textbooks, product-based learning objectives that are *about* the subject matter are the single largest deterrent to teaching critical-thinking skills.

Product-based learning objectives came about as a consequence of applying Frederick Taylor's (1919) scientific management and measurement theories to education. Taylor's ideas, which in their early form gave rise to the "efficiency expert," were based *in part* on the belief that human work could be measured in much the same way that one measures the output of a machine—so many pieces per hour. He understood that while methodology and measurement went together, method was paramount. From his vantage point on the second floor of a factory, Taylor began his great life's work by observing men carrying iron ingots from the factory door to a railroad siding some distance away. Watching the work patterns, Taylor made changes in how they went about their tasks. In other words, he did not start with measuring; he started, instead, by observing methodology with a view towards improving it. Measuring entered the picture later as a means of assessing the effect of *changes* in method.

According to R.E. Callahan (1962, p. 244), the educational problems we have imposed on ourselves and our students stem not from the borrowing of the principles of scientific management but from their misapplication. Educators have reversed Taylor's principles, adopting the idea that the output of teachers and students can be improved through measurement without changing the prevailing teaching and learning method (i.e. lecture-for-recall), a change that would make measuring meaningful. This backwards idea is at odds with Taylor's scientific manage-

Product-based learning objectives that are about the subject matter are the single largest deterrent to teaching critical-thinking skills.

ment principle: primary concern for methodology over measurement. Assessment programs that concentrate on outcomes, without primary concern for the teaching and learning *methodology* that produce the outcomes, are ultimately devoid of educational value.

Teachers who teach *about* subject matter tend to be overwhelmed by the sheer bulk of subject matter that they are expected to "cover." Too many confuse "teaching" with "covering" subject matter. In our era of the information explosion, the teacher's main job is no longer to communicate a body of knowledge, but rather to teach students how to analyze and evaluate available knowledge. Teachers' prime concern is guiding students in the development and exercise of their cognitive skills so that they can master what they find out. How can teachers do their job best? Within what pedagogical framework can the subject matter be delivered? With what regard for developing thinking skills? With what thinking-skills outcomes? These critical considerations disappear as relevant issues in classrooms when teachers merely "cover" the material.

Through workshops I have conducted on means-ends methodology, I have come to understand the extreme demands placed upon grade-school teachers. Public-school teachers experience pressures that post-secondary teachers rarely, if ever, feel. The official curricula require that stated, large amounts of content must be processed in very little time. This millwork, factory approach causes teachers to emphasize rote learning; the teaching and learning of thinking skills are assigned a low, or non-existent, priority. This assembly-line approach to schooling discourages innovation, shortchanges students, and generates a false sense of accomplishment. The time has come, however, when less is more. Less emphasis on merely covering content can mean more time and effort spent in teaching and learning critical skills.

In our era of the information explosion, the teacher's main job is no longer to communicate a body of knowledge, but rather to teach students how to analyze and evaluate available knowledge. Teachers' prime concern is guiding students in the development and exercise of their cognitive skills so that they can master what they find out.

One of the consequences of teaching *about* rather than from *within* subject matter is that it deprives us of a *conscious* concern for developing critical-thinking skills. When training preservice or inservice teachers, we emphasize the necessary skills associated with superior organization and presentation, writing objectives, selecting appropriate educational technology, preparation and delivery of lesson plans, and assessment of student achievement. But there is a catch: We do this in the context of teaching *about*, not from *within*, subject matter. We send out generation after generation of newly certified teachers who continue to practice a form of teaching that induces rote learning instead of critical thinking.

We Are Limited in Our Awareness of the Need for Instruction in Cognitive Skills

A national study conducted by the National Center for Research to Improve Post-secondary Teaching and Learning (NCRIPTAL 1989, p. 2) found that many teachers "see their fields as organized bodies of knowledge to transmit...[or] skills to learn and apply." The majority are unaware that they actually need to teach thinking skills. The teacher is concerned primarily with planning. The conscious development of critical-thinking skills is not an operational consideration. Yet, the same NCRIPTAL study found that "faculty overwhelmingly believe that the purpose of education is to think effectively."

The self-contradictory mindset of teachers who realize that critical thinking is important, but who do not know how to promote critical-thinking skills in students, "dovetails perfectly with the passive attitude of most students. Most are unprepared...to think critically....They assume...the textbook...or the professor will tell them what they are to do or say. Hence, even though the professor may think that critical thinking is being required, most students will not produce it for the simple reason that they don't know how." (Paul, 1989, p. 8)

English and philosophy faculties are generally more aware of the problems associated with developing thinking because of their traditional involvement in dealing with cognitive skills. But it is my experience that they see critical thinking in the context of formal logic and Socratic questioning and not in the context of discussing content across the curriculum. Some colleges and universities have sought to extend the teaching of these skills beyond the traditional departments by implementing college-wide programs. King's College in Wilkes-Barre, Pennsylvania, has a program to prepare faculty members "in all departments...to become familiar with the [core] critical thinking course and with specific strategies for developing students' thinking skills in a conscious way across the curriculum." (Hammerbacher, p. 2, 1990) Alverno College in Milwaukee, Wisconsin, operates under the principle that "critical thinking needs to be systematically taught and learned in every subject area." (Cromwell, 1990, p. 1)

For the most part, however, teachers and administrators at all academic levels are oriented primarily to using textbooks, rote presentations, and collecting enrollment and financial data. While they may be aware of the term "critical thinking," they are not aware of its implications with respect to the *classroom* teaching and learning of subject matter. Educators use terms associated with cognitive skills (analysis, evaluation, problem-solving), without recognizing that a corresponding methodological revolution must take place if these skills are to be taught and learned. An example of this is the increasingly widespread and odious practice of textbook authors who relabel end-of-chapter questions as "Critical Thinking Exercises" without any corresponding change in their text that would place the subject matter they describe within a critical-thinking context. Unfortunately, many educators who use such texts are misled to believe that they are now developing cognitive skills in students.

We are concerned with saving the underprepared student, challenging the prepared student, and reconceptualizing teacher eduction. We are concerned with bringing critical-thinking skills to everyday activities, to the family, to the community, and to the workplace. We are concerned with allowing students to develop their cognitive skills so that they may rescue themselves from the banality of much that is modern culture. We are concerned with educating a thoughtful citizenry that can preserve and protect the democratic way of life.

The use of terms such as "reflective thought," "problem solving," and the "scientific method" in an educational context was made popular through the writings of John Dewey. (1916, 1933) These terms are commonly used today by many educators at all levels; however, "school teachers and university professors have gained a superficial acquaintance with Dewey's terminology without reflecting upon the implications of those terms." (Shermis, 1992) Educators have yet to recognize that use of the terminology must be accompanied by teaching and learning methodologies that would make the terms come alive and provide real, critical, meaning for teachers and students alike. They have yet to recognize that a real methodological problem exists. If method is destiny, then lecture-for-recall destines teachers and students alike to a lifetime of rote, not critical, thinking, teaching, and learning.

There are other implications as well. The general lack of awareness of what critical thinking is, and how it may be taught across the curriculum, redounds throughout the higher education arena. We must at least be aware of what is at stake for the student. It affects the determination of institutional missions, program planning and budgeting, and educational technology, including the selection of textbooks, instructional software, inservice training, faculty development, articulation, and grant funding. We are concerned with saving the underprepared student, challenging the prepared student, and reconceptualizing teacher eduction. We are concerned with bringing critical-thinking skills to everyday activities, to the family, to the community, and to the workplace. We are concerned with allowing students to develop their cognitive skills so that they may rescue themselves from the banality of much that is modern culture. We are concerned with educating a thoughtful citizenry that can preserve and protect the democratic way of life. The more we require students to listen to lectures, memorize textbook material, and take objective exams with built-in answers, the less they think critically, and the less sure we are that our society's concerns will be addressed and met.

We throw up roadblocks to learning when we confuse organization with methodology, rely on textbooks, underestimate subject matter, teach *about* the subject matter rather than *within* the subject matter itself, and are unaware of the need for curriculum-wide instruction in cognitive skills. All these factors conspire to perpetuate the lecture method and the rote learning it induces.

New Affirmations of Critical Thinking in the Classroom

Given the long-standing hold of the lecture method and the barriers to change described above, is there any hope that thinking across the curriculum can become as widespread as is the lecture-for-recall method? Can the situation be turned around? Can we produce teachers who understand and teach critical thinking? Can critical thinking be taught in the classroom regardless of subject matter?

The answer to all these questions is "yes," if we can affirm the following:

- a commitment to the concept of critical thinking across the curriculum

- an effective methodological understanding of what critical thinking comprises

- an understanding of some important distinctions, including the difference between organization and methodology

- an appreciation of how the lecture-for-recall method and conventional textbooks induce rote-learning

- an appreciation that all subject matter is dynamic, and that when we seek merely to memorize it, we diminish it and our intellectual selves

- an understanding that learning objectives get in the way of appreciating the dynamics of subject matter because objectives are *about* the subject matter rather than drawn from *within* the subject matter itself

- an understanding that cognitive skills must be consciously taught, and that students must share in the conscious engagement with critical skills

- a realization that we penalize both the prepared and underprepared student when we teach for recall instead of for critical skills

- an across-the-curriculum methodology that will allow teachers to deliver the subject matter itself while simultaneously developing cognitive skills

4 Attributes of an Effective Methodology for Teaching Critical Thinking

Criteria for an Ideal Teaching Method

If current teaching methods are ineffective in promoting critical skills, why not design a new approach to teaching? When I became aware that I needed to become a teacher of critical-thinking skills, I set myself the task of imagining an ideal teaching method. The following list of criteria is what I came up with:

- Course content (subject matter) and critical thinking are to be taught simultaneously.

- The subject matter, not the teacher, is the focal point of the classroom.

- The students must become actively involved in manipulating the subject matter.

- An ideal method works in all subject matter disciplines.

- An ideal method works both in introductory courses and at advanced learning levels.

- An ideal method works with all forms of educational technology.

- An ideal method works outside of the classroom setting as well as within the classroom.

- An ideal method provides a practical basis for assessing achievement.

Simultaneity

Teaching course content and subject matter at the same time allows traditional subject matter to be taught in a manner that promotes critical-thinking skills. Teaching in this way merges process with product; the product of thinking and the process of thinking become the two aspects of a cognitive whole. Teaching that uses a critical method of subject matter delivery (the process) allows students to achieve a critical understanding of that subject matter (the product).

Here is an example that involves simultaneity: A few years back, I attended a meeting on teaching for critical thinking. The speaker provided exercises that demonstrated how teachers could help students differentiate a fact from an inference. When an audience member (a teacher of biology) asked how one would apply the exercises to teaching biology, the speaker threw up his hands and shrugged his shoulders. The speaker's ideas would work only in isolation from subject matter. In order to use the speaker's ideas, the teacher would be expected to stop his or her discussion of regular course content, detour into an abstract discussion of facts and inferences, and then return to discussing regular course content. This is what I mean by the divorce of process from product. With this approach, simultaneity is not possible.

Approaches to teaching critical thinking that lack simultaneity send exactly the wrong message to both teacher and student, namely, that teaching critical skills and learning to think critically bear no relationship to the subject matter currently being taught and learned; that critical thinking is not something one can do in the classroom, with a textbook, or while studying. All of these false statements, nonetheless, represent the prevailing view and practice.

A methodology that simultaneously joins process with product would be at once both a teaching and a learning methodology, and it would accomplish the following:

- Method, content, and the development of critical skills are unified.

- Teachers and students see that all subject matter discussed in a classroom can be engaged critically.

- Any topic, in or out of the classroom, can be engaged critically.

- Teachers and students become partners in the critical analysis of subject matter.

Focus

Making the subject matter itself, rather than the teacher and pedagogical purposes, the focus of the classroom effort, directs the students' attention to where it belongs, to the content of the subject matter. The students take a more active role in learning, and the teacher can concentrate on the root meaning of "education," to lead the learner to knowledge.

The prevailing use of the lecture-for-recall method guarantees that the teacher, not the subject matter, will be the center of student attention. Despite pre-school experiences wherein children, in effect, teach themselves many of the skills necessary for dealing with their world, students, upon entering school, quickly gather that if a teacher doesn't say it, they can't—or won't—learn it. The spontaneous growth in self-sufficiency at learning that children bring to the classroom is arrested, diminished, and eventually lost because the teacher, and not the subject matter to be learned, becomes the major force in the learning environment. This perception of learning, established in grade school, continues through to high school, college, university, and graduate school.

One way to focus on subject matter is to discuss material critically. The most common approach to classroom discussion is dialectical discourse. Under the proper

The spontaneous growth in self-sufficiency at learning that children bring to the classroom is arrested, diminished, and eventually lost because the teacher, and not the subject matter to be learned, becomes the major force in the learning environment.

conditions, this Socratic style of questioning can yield excellent results; however, in most classroom situations, engaging students in dialectics places most of the burden for thinking critically on the teacher. Because the teacher knows more, and has already reflected critically on the subject, the effect is to have the teacher do all the thinking. This reduces the students to silence, or else the teacher plays a sort of game, pretending not to know, while attempting to pull intelligent comments out of uninformed students. Even though subject matter is critically engaged by the discussion leader posing appropriate questions, the teacher nevertheless becomes a barrier between the student and critical analysis of the subject matter. Allowing the subject matter itself, rather than the teacher, to be the focal point of discussion resolves this Socratic breakdown.

A teaching and learning methodology that includes a critical focus accomplishes the following:

- Because the subject matter, and not the teacher, is the focal point of the classroom, students are required to take a more active role in learning.

- Students experience the subject matter directly.

- Students' over-reliance on teachers ("Just tell us what you want us to know!") is minimized. Students learn to engage subject matter independently, without the constant aid of a teacher.

- The basis for developing lifelong learning skills is established.

Involvement

Requiring the active participation of students causes them to engage the subject matter directly, and it places the responsibility for learning where it ultimately belongs— on the students themselves.

Students are routinely denied active involvement with their learning because of the prevailing use of the lecture-for-recall method and the rote learning it induces. The implications for American education are serious when students remain intellectually passive in the classroom. The failure of student involvement, motivation, persistence, and achievement have been at the heart of several national studies, e.g. *A Nation at Risk* (1983), *Action for Excellence* (1983), *Involvement in Learning* (1984), and *American Education—Making it Work* (1988).

When achieved, the involvement criterion helps further to professionalize teaching. For perhaps the first time, teachers, like doctors, lawyers, and engineers, come to posses specific, valuable skills, not merely the ability to deliver or profess well-worn subject matter; all teachers become teachers of critical thinking.

Multidisciplinarity

The ability of all teachers to apply the method in all disciplines allows teachers all across the curriculum to teach critical-thinking skills.

While some approaches work better than others in some subjects, an inter- and multidisciplinary approach is the metacognitive method that allows many fields and many methods to inform one another. A multidisciplinary approach provides the basis for perceiving all subject matter as possessing and sharing certain dynamic elements. All subject matter is shown to be cognitively interconnected, not isolated knowledge crystals bearing no intellectual or functional relationships. A multidisciplinary approach that emphasizes what is common in subject matter allows educators to see new ways of working together and new ways of drawing on the strengths and special insights that their areas of knowledge offer. Carried into the classroom, a multidisciplinary approach provides new ways for students to appreciate that one knowledge area informs another. An interconnected view of knowledge leads to a similarly unified view of the world, prompting students to understand that people, ideas, life, nature, and society are likewise interrelated. A multidisciplinary approach promotes the development of cognitive skills because every teacher in every classroom becomes able to discuss subject matter within a critical, thoughtful framework.

All levels

Applicability of the method both in introductory courses and at advanced learning levels allows students at all levels to begin to develop thinking skills the first time they are introduced to a new subject-matter field, and to continue them thereafter.

A properly staged methodology allows teachers to forsake the widely held impression that students must first be lectured on a new topic before they can be asked to think critically about that topic; critical thinking begins at the lowest possible grade level.

A method usable at every stage of learning remains as timely later on at a more advanced stage as it was earlier at the beginners' stage. The more a subject is engaged intellectually, the more likely will a critical and contextual understanding be assembled.

Commonality

Applicability of the method to a variety of educational technologies helps assure that all forms of subject-matter delivery take place in a critical-thinking context.

If textbooks presented subject matter in a way that promoted critical thinking, then animating these texts would surely be an excellent achievement, but conventional textbooks do not promote critical thinking; they promote rote learning. The rote-inducing influence of the textbook format extends even beyond the classroom because it has been taken as a model of presentation by authors of computer courseware. Like an oil spill, the textbook format mentality has contaminated pristine technological areas and clogged imaginative approaches.

Microcomputer technology is a sad example. Although the literature reveals some innovative and exciting instructional uses of microcomputer technology, most of the evidence indicates that the traditional textbook-based mindset is being perpetrated by software and courseware writers. "Project Socrates" at Cornell University, for example, is aimed at finding and connecting the elements common to all engineering disciplines. In engineering work, "No single line graph or color image can convey the complex, evolving interactions [that occur in design]. Since we cannot put such animation into a textbook, why not put the textbook into an animator [workstation]?" (Ingraffea and Minks, 1988, p. 60). To adopt textbook methodology as an instructional design, merely to set a textbook in motion—in essence, to televise it—is shortsighted, old-fashioned, and it limits the computer's potential, depriving educators of a powerful learning tool for teaching thinking skills. An ideal method would allow all forms of educational technology to deliver their subject matter within a critical-thinking context.

Transferability

The ability to use the thinking skills learned inside of the classroom outside of the classroom makes the goals of lifelong learning and workplace competency a reality.

Transferability "has been elusive—the bane of most instructional programs aimed at developing thinkers." (Siegal & Carey, 1989, p. 12) Gaining the skills of critical thought is for a longer-term effect than enhancing achievement and persistence while in school and college only. The transfer of critical skills to other areas of life, such as the family, the workplace, and the community, helps students become grownups who make independent analyses and evaluations.

For example, the ability to think, read, write, listen, and speak—critically and for oneself—is at the center of functional democracy; these basic skills are, in effect, the human tools of democracy. The increasingly widespread lack of these skills and their use threatens America's democratic institutions and thwarts the development of democracies the world over. The teacher of critical thinking is a teacher who promotes democratic ideals, principles, and practices.

Teachers, curriculum designers, educational technologists, and administrators at all academic levels must seriously combat over-reliance on teaching methodologies that promote passive acceptance of pre-packaged ideas, crystallized conceptions of subject matter that allow for narrow-mindedness, and limits on the ability of students to make independent analyses and value judgments.

One can see that "thinking across the curriculum"—transferability—has implications that transcend the campus classroom.

A methodology that accomplishes transferability makes the teaching of thinking skills in the classroom a vital link with a student's family, social, and career responsibilities, and civic participation. Transferable critical-thinking skills strengthen our democratic society.

Assessability

A thoughtful and shared instrument by which to measure progress provides both teacher and student with the ability to evaluate mutually what has been learned.

Traditional assessment instruments that assume the use of traditional teaching methodology help to perpetuate lecture-for-recall and a lack of critical thought. Furthermore, merely adding to assessment instruments test items aimed at evaluating cognitive skills is nearly pointless when these skills are not taught in all classrooms in a systematic and across-the-curriculum manner.

An ideal method not only informs the teacher of a student's progress but also it informs the *student* as well. Because the ideal method merges process with product (simultaneity), students become able to determine their state of learning and which areas require attention.

A Review of Existing Methodologies

Three classroom teaching methodologies are now in use: the lecture, Socratic questioning, and systematic problem-solving. In this section, I review each of these; in the following section, I compare them to the criteria of an ideal methodology as stated above.

The Lecture

Although, according to a study conducted by the National Center for Research to Improve Post-secondary Teaching and Learning, "faculty overwhelmingly believe that the purpose of education is to think effectively" (NCRIPTAL, 1989, p. 2), the lecture method is the road followed by most classroom teachers in the delivery of subject matter, and the ruts are deep. That road began in Sicily around 450 B.C.E. as the art of rhetoric, and it goes ever on to this day in many forms, including the classroom lecture.

> Today, the lecture method is preferred by most professors. With few exceptions, when we visited classes, the teacher stood in front of rows of chairs and talked most of the forty-five or fifty minutes. Information was presented that students often passively received. There was little opportunity for positions to be clarified or ideas to be challenged. (Boyer, 1987)

The lecture format has a strong academic tradition and it has served the *faculty* well. It is used when time is short, when a large amount of content needs to be covered, and when the class size is large. Unfortunately, in terms of teaching cognitive skills (as well as reading, writing, listening, and speaking skills that are informed by cognitive skills), these conditions and restraints are all too common in many elementary-school, high-school, and college classrooms. The lecture format is the most popular approach to classroom teaching for at least these reasons:

The lecture format has a strong academic tradition and it has served the faculty well...The lecture method, nevertheless, has not been kind to students.

- The lecture method is traditional, and tradition carries its own logic.

- Lecture is the only methodology known to most teachers.

- Lecture can be easily adopted by those new to teaching.

- Lecture lends itself to objective test items.

- Because many teachers closely follow the assigned text, the sequential presentation of topics in textbooks and other forms of educational technology conform to, and reinforce, the lecture method.

The lecture method, nevertheless, has not been kind to students. I discuss the limitations of the lecture method in chapter 1, and I summarize here its limitations in developing students' critical-thinking skills

- Topics are discussed sequentially, not critically, thus depriving both student and teacher of a dynamic understanding of the subject matter. A dynamic understanding of the subject matter includes the critical ability to see the underlying structure that supports all subject-matter areas.

- Presented with lectures, students make a logical decision to memorize the material (learn by rote). They can see no practical alternative to a method that stresses the sequential, classroom, and textbook delivery of large amounts of subject matter.

- Students become passive under the lecture method. The teacher does most of the talking, questioning, answering, and therefore most of the thinking.

- Lectures do not address basic and critical thinking, reading, writing, and speaking skills, and it teaches students to listen passively.

- Underprepared students are placed at a significant disadvantage because they generally possess poor rote-learning skills.

- Even well-prepared students do not grow intellectually.

- The lecture method does not allow teachers or students to assess the state of critical comprehension of subject matter.

Two little-used methodologies have been available to those teachers concerned with teaching subject matter and critical skills at the same time: Socratic questioning and problem-solving.

Socratic Questioning

The asking of questions in an attempt to probe the validity of an argument, viewpoint, or proposition is generally attributed to Socrates (ca. 470—399 B.C.E.). Socratic questioning, or the critical method, is known by many other names including "expansion questioning," "critical questioning," "dialogical and dialectical discourse," "productive questioning," and "progressive questioning."

One approach to the critical method is through the adaptation of learning taxonomies like those of Bloom's hierarchy of thinking skills, Piaget's developmental hierarchy, and Paul's categories of critical thinking. These taxonomies serve as a basis for an instructional method, variously known as "expansion questioning," "higher-order questing," "dialectical questioning," and "dialogical questioning." They are all aimed at developing critical-thinking skills in students: Teachers ask questions that take the student up through the taxonomic levels. This kind of questioning is most valuable when the class size is very small (probably five or fewer), the subject covered is narrowly defined, and ample time is available; however, these conditions do not exist in most classrooms.

Going beyond Socrates

The limitations of methodologies based on the Socratic style are as follows:

- The student must have had prior exposure to the subject matter.

- Most of the responsibility for questioning (that is, thinking critically), is placed on the teacher, not on the student.

- By relying on the teacher to ask the questions, students do not engage in question-posing, an essential aspect of critical thinking.

- Effectiveness of the Socratic method relies on working with small groups of students over an extended period.

- The Socratic method severely limits the amount of content that may be critically engaged.

- The dialogical style is used primarily in the language arts and the humanities and practically not at all in the sciences, engineering, and career areas, where many students concentrate their studies.

- The Socratic method provides a weak foundation for across-the-curriculum assessment efforts.

Systematic Problem-solving

The procedural steps involved in the modern problem-solving process stem from the reflective-thought constructs of John Dewey (see Chapter 3). Here are some examples of how problem-solving is used in classrooms:

- working in mathematics, George Polya described this problem-solving process: Understand the problem, devise a plan, carry out a plan, and look back (in Greenfield, 1987, p. 10).

- Woods (1987, p. 55) described this option for teaching problem-solving, and Meyers (1986, pp. 4 and 23) described a procedure that parallels the one described by Woods: Start with a problem, read about the situation, define the situation/problem, define the "real" problem and devise a representation, make a plan, do the plan, check, look back, implement, arrive at solution.

- Stonewater (1980, p. 33) described a guided design approach used at West Virginia University: Encourage students to identify problems, list constraints and assumptions, and generate alternative solutions.

Assuming knowledge of the process itself, the problem-solving method is most effective when used to address problems in a field with which the student already possesses some knowledge and understanding. Many (maybe most) teachers, researchers, and writers involved with problem-solving are concerned with teaching the problem-solving process itself, not with using a problem-solving approach to teach course subject matter. When used to discuss subject matter (as in the case-study method), students must have first gained an initial understanding of the topics under study. The case-study method has its greatest application at the upper and graduate levels of university.

Limitations of the problem-solving approach are as follows:

- The problem-solving method requires that students understand the problem-solving process itself.

- Problem-solving requires existing knowledge of the subject matter in which the problem is framed.

- By being presented with ready-made problems to solve, the student does not engage in problem-posing, an essential aspect of critical thinking.

- Problem-solving lends itself well to math and the sciences but practically not at all to other disciplines.

Based on the criteria for an ideal method of critical thinking, I present in the following table a comparison of existing teaching methodologies. The column labeled "Socratic ques-

Existing Methodologies and an Ideal Method: A Comparison

tioning" represents all those questioning techniques that require the teacher to take and maintain the lead in questioning. An ideal method would, by definition, score excellent in all categories. I base the ratings of the other methods on the foregoing discussion. You are welcome to rate the methods according to your own perceptions of their usefulness. I believe that while you might move this or that method up or down a notch, the general conclusion, that existing methodologies are poor choices for critical thinking across the curriculum, will be borne out. I invite you to rate my own method, MECA/SM, after you have finished reading this book.

Teaching Method Attributes	Ideal Method	Lecture	Socratic Question-ing	Problem-solving	MECA/SM
Simultaneity (Teach subject matter and cognitive skills simultaneously)	Excellent	Poor	Poor	Poor	
Focus (Subject matter is focus of classroom)	Excellent	Fair	Good	Good	
Involvement (Active learning)	Excellent	Poor	Fair	Good	
Multidisciplinary (Works in all disciplines)	Excellent	Excellent	Poor	Good	
All Levels (Works in introductory courses and at advanced levels)	Excellent	Excellent	Fair	Fair	
Commonality (Works with all forms of educational technology)	Excellent	Excellent	Fair	Fair	
Transferability (Works outside the classroom)	Excellent	Poor	Poor	Fair	
Assessability (Student can assess state of learning)	Excellent	Poor	Poor	Fair	

The table shows that all three existing methodologies fall short of meeting the stated criteria. In discussing methodology, Shermis wrote: "[W]hile many teachers are undoubtedly sincere in their desire to encourage students to think, they typically have had few, if any, models in their experience who exemplified open-ended, inquiry-oriented, critical thinking. Teachers teach as they have been taught. Thus despite the thin veneer acquired in methods classes in teacher-education programs, most teachers lack philosophical assumptions relevant to, and teaching strategies consistent with, an inquiry approach to learning." (1992, p. 12) I conclude that we suffer from a major lack of critical-thinking teaching strategies. Whereas scholars have "heartily theorized about the nature of critical thinking, none of them has presented a thorough but practical model to guide teachers." (Smith, 1990, p. 43) Notice that Smith established two requirements: The method must be (a) thorough, and it must be (b) practical.

Developing a thorough and practical methodology that involves simultaneity, focus, involvement, multi-disciplinarity, all levels, commonality, transferability, and assessability, has great implications for teaching critical-thinking skills across the curriculum, and it is obviously an extremely tall order. In chapters 5 through 9, I introduce a new strategy for engaging subject matter, and I propose an approach that involves thinking, teaching, learning, and subject matter all together at once within a critical-thinking framework. I call my new strategy Means-Ends Critical Analysis of Subject Matter (MECA/SM). Once you have gained an understanding of MECA/SM and have actually applied it to your own field, you will be in a position to complete the last column in the foregoing table. I invite you to see if the requirements of thoroughness and practicality have been met.

A New Method for Thinking across the Curriculum

5 Introduction to Means-Ends Critical Analysis of Subject Matter

Means-Ends Critical Analysis of Subject Matter is a methodology that allows one to teach any subject matter and critical thinking at the same time.

That subject matter and critical thinking can be taught at the same time is not an idea that is easily accepted. Many teachers operate under the assumption that students must first hear lectures on a subject before they can think about it. The notion is that unless certain knowledge-based objectives are met first, students will not have the proper background to address issues and questions that require analysis and evaluation. This preoccupation with transmitting information, when added to the sheer amount of facts and truths that most teachers are expected to deliver, however, deals a double blow to the classroom development of thinking skills: 1) Because knowledge must precede thinking, thinking cannot be addressed simultaneously. 2) Because there is so much content to be covered, thinking must wait for some other time or forum. The result is that critical thinking remains permanently on a back burner. Consider this dialogue between a teacher and a critical thinker:

MECA/SM

Teacher (lamenting):

My students must know certain facts, and I have to lecture to them about these facts. Don't they first have to *know something* before I can more fully engage their minds?

Critical Thinker:

What subject do you teach?

Teacher:

Biology.

Critical Thinker:

And how do you start a typical lesson?

Teacher:

I tell the class that "Today we are going to discuss the cell"—or whatever the topic happens to be.

Critical Thinker:

I have a suggestion for you. Instead of starting by talking *about* what you and your class are going to do, saying "Today we are going to discuss the cell," start the lesson instead by telling them something that is drawn from *within* the subject matter itself. Start by saying "The purpose of the cell is to serve as the basic building block for living things. Today we are going to find out how that purpose is achieved." Then develop your discussion by using means-ends critical analysis. You will cover the same material that you usually cover, and your students will be exposed to the same knowledge that you usually deliver, but there will be one major difference: You will have delivered your material in a critical-thinking context. In so doing, you will be simultaneously covering subject matter and developing critical-thinking skills in your students.

Means-Ends Critical Analysis of Subject Matter (MECA/SM) involves establishing the purpose of the subject matter under discussion, identifying the means needed to achieve the purposes established (means constitute resources *plus* the activities in which the resources are employed), and evaluating the results (consequences) of achieving the purpose. Ponder the two following examples that illustrate how subject matter is analyzed and presented when using means-ends analysis. The first is based on analyzing a text, the second is based on analyzing one's own experience.

A Typical Text-based Analysis

Consider this particularly well-written passage which includes not only elements of purpose, resource, and activities but also results as well.

> In May of 1796 [Dr. Edward Jenner] selected an eight-year-old boy and inoculated him with "matter taken from the sore hand of a dairymaid." The next day the boy became ill—fever, headache, loss of appetite—but the following day he was completely well again. Several months later Jenner inoculated the child with "matter" taken from a smallpox pustule. The child was protected; no disease occurred. The experiment was a success, and the human species (and their domestic animals) began to secure the protection of immunization. (Desowitz, 1987, p. 24)

According to a means-ends analysis of this passage, I arrange the material in the paragraph to show its purpose. Notice the following about the illustration below: The essential meaning of the passage has been identified and placed under *Purpose*. The means used to achieve the purpose have been identified and separated according to their nature: Static means appear under *Resources*, and dynamic means appear under *Activities*. The results of achieving the purpose appear under *Consequences*.

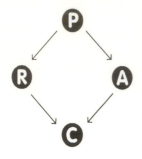

Title: A Means-Ends Analysis
of the Immunization Passage

PURPOSE

to protect the boy from disease

RESOURCES

- Dr. Edward Jenner
- dairymaid
- "matter" from maid's sore hand
- eight-year-old boy
- smallpox pustule

ACTIVITIES

- boy inoculated with "matter" from dairymaid's hand
- boy became ill
- boy recovered next day
- boy later inoculated with "matter" from smallpox pustule
- no disease occurred in boy

CONSEQUENCES

Human species and domestic animals
gained the protection of immunization.

All of the elements were drawn from the quoted passage. This kind of analysis makes textbook subject matter come alive; it is not just a recitation of names and dates. The purpose, means, and consequences inherent in the information has been portrayed graphically.

Not all passages contain the four basic parts that constitute a means-ends analysis. Reasonably complete and well-written paragraphs should contain at least the elements of purpose, resource, and activity; results or consequences, as in the present example, are occasionally included. The lack of any part, or incomplete treatments, however, does not prevent an analysis from being made. Associated paragraphs can be analyzed for supplemental information. Once the material at hand has been sorted out, the analyst can evaluate the portrayal as to its completeness and logical connectivity. Means-ends analysis can go far beyond paragraph treatments. By analyzing topic headings and the first sentences in each associated paragraph, it is possible to develop a means-ends analysis of an entire textbook chapter. It is not necessary, however, to evaluate a textual passage in order to perform a means-ends analysis. One's own existing knowledge and understanding of some subject can serve as the basis for an analysis.

I was invited to address a City University of New York ad-hoc committee on the nursing curriculum (New York City Office of Academic Affairs, April 20, 1990.) I wanted to illustrate for the committee members how means-ends analysis could be used on their subject matter. I contacted the Nursing Department at the College, and there I made the acquaintance of Professor Alexandria Tarasko.

I explained the means-ends concept, and over the next two days Professor Tarasko and I developed several analyses on various topics. The following analysis about blood is significant because it is not based on any textbook, but, rather, was developed on the basis of Professor Tarasko's knowledge and understanding of her field.

A Typical Experience-based Analysis

Title: Means-Ends Analysis of the Function of Blood

PURPOSE

to deliver oxygen and other nutrients to body tissue;
to rid the body of waste material

RESOURCES	ACTIVITIES
• effective heart	• food, oxygen taken in
• patent arteries	• food broken down, oxygen diffused
• appropriate diet	• blood picks up nutrients and oxygen
• oxygen	• blood delivers nutrients and oxygen to tissues
• clear airways	• waste products are picked up by blood
	• blood delivers waste products to elimination system and lungs

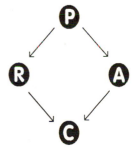

CONSEQUENCES

If the purposes are achieved, body tissue is
maintained and repaired; if not, tissues die.

They discover that the ability to think critically already resides within them-selves.

MECA/SM and Subject Matter

When the analyses were shown to the members of the ad-hoc committee, they were able to relate means-ends analysis to their own existing interests and knowl-edge. Performing analyses based on one's experience is an effective way to introduce anyone, including teachers, to means-ends analysis of subject matter. Because an experience-based analysis requires only what is presently known and understood, it can be used to introduce means-ends analysis to high-school and college students. Introductions of the means-ends approach made in this fashion allow students to demonstrate and appreciate their own existing knowledge; then, they demonstrate to themselves and to the teacher that they can, indeed, think critically. They discover that the ability to think critically already resides within themselves.

The term "material" as used in this discussion refers to subject matter as it is expressed in facts, ideas, issues, points-of-view, beliefs, feelings, principles, arguments, claims, theories, thoughts, situations, procedures, inter-pretations, policies, perspectives, assumptions, infer-ences, predictions, and evidence. The term "textbook" refers to the normal printed representation of subject matter, but in the context of this discussion it also refers to audio, video, film, and computer representations.

Means-ends analysis is concerned with obtaining a critical understanding of material that the thinker has ei-ther already internalized or material that is new. In the case of existing knowledge, one performs a means-ends analysis so that one may critically reconstruct what was learned by rote. If you are a teacher, you will analyze new material for critical presentation in class. If you are a student, you will reconstruct new material presented through classroom lecture, or as it is presented in text-book and other resources.

Critical thinkers realize that material is always presented egocentrically and sociocentrically. This means that subject matter is invariably presented within the context of the presenter's life experiences, preferences, and biases. A means-ends representation can provide the basis for determining whether these filters have the effect of making the textbook or other material incomplete, incorrect, outdated, or misleading. The material in a textbook is a combination of the author's preferences and the important ideas and issues associated with the curriculum area that the author represents. Therefore, a means-ends analysis provides a representation of material portrayed through the interpretive filters of individuals and groups. Because every presenter is a member of some group, the material is likely also to be suffused with that group's beliefs, policies, and perspectives. Textbooks are good examples of these forces at play.

Because MECA/SM includes analysis of consequences (results) along with analysis of means and ends, a means-ends approach provides the basis for addressing and developing, in teachers and students alike, all those cognitive skills generally associated with critical thinking. Once one understands what is given, one can proceed to make informative evaluations, engage in dialogue, and seek alternatives. The great power of means-ends analysis is its ability to structure one's critical understanding of material as it is initially encountered, and to lay the foundation for evaluating consequences. The analyst has the ability to determine whether or not a particular analysis is a fair representation of the subject matter at hand, and to evaluate likely consequences.

A key to determining the likelihood of distortion, misrepresentation, or propagandizing lies in whether the material under analysis is information-loaded or rhetoric-loaded. Particularly with textbooks, the more the material is information-loaded, the less likely is the threat that gross distortions will appear. The more the material is

Because every presenter is a member of some group, then the material is likely also to be suffused with that group's beliefs, policies, and perspectives. Textbooks are good examples of these forces at play.

A means-ends representation can provide the basis for determining whether these filters have the effect of making the textbook or other material to be incomplete, incorrect, outdated, or misleading.

loaded with rhetoric, the greater the possibility that unsupported biases and prejudices will surface. MECA/SM helps one make this determination because it prompts the analyst to determine whether the stated or implied purpose in the material at hand is properly supported by the means cited.

Information-loaded versus Rhetoric-loaded Material

Information-loaded Subject Matter

When subject matter is information-loaded, disagreement regarding its interpretation is less likely to occur. Here are some examples upon which informed people tend to agree:

- Mathematics: the area of a triangle is obtained by taking one-half of the product of the triangle's base and height dimensions.

- Physics: force is calculated by multiplying mass by acceleration.

- Electrical Engineering: voltage is calculated by multiplying current by resistance.

- Accounting: gross profit is determined by subtracting costs from revenues.

- Marketing: a product's market potential can be estimated by conducting (among other things) a demographic analysis.

- Nursing: the process of nursing includes collecting data, analyzing data, formulating a diagnosis, deciding on realistic goals and outcomes, planning appropriate interventions, and evaluating the effectiveness of the interventions.

Textbooks in the physical sciences, mathematics, technologies, and career areas are primarily information-loaded. This does not mean that they are free of bias, prejudice, or misrepresentation. It does mean that means-ends analysis is likely to provide the analyst with a fairly comprehensive critical understanding of the subject matter analyzed. For this reason, means-ends critical analysis of subject matter allows one to teach and learn subject matter and critical thinking at the same time while retaining reasonable confidence that the material analyzed will result in a fair-minded representation.

Rhetoric-loaded Subject Matter

When subject matter is rhetoric-loaded, disagreement is more likely to arise regarding interpretations and the points-of-view expressed. Here are some examples upon which disagreement is likely:

- There is a supreme being controlling our destinies.

- Capitalism is the best form of economic organization.

- Laboratory experiments with animals are justified.

- The earth's atmosphere is warming.

- Abortions are acceptable.

- Darwin's theory of evolution is scientific and largely correct.

Textbooks in philosophy, social sciences, and language arts are more problematic from both a teaching and a learning standpoint because the material they contain is inescapably fertile ground for multiple interpretations. Nonetheless, means-ends analysis is still powerful in these areas because it allows the analyst critically to understand the elements that constitute the arguments being made and the ideas being offered. In these cases, means-ends analysis provides the crucial basis for further discussion and investigation because the subsequent dialogue will be based on a clear understanding of initial viewpoints or representations that are under dialogical discussion. Further discussion, along Socratic lines, of rhetoric-loaded issues is more likely to prove fruitful when initial positions are clearly understood.

Of course, most books and discussions are combinations of information and rhetoric. MECA/SM strategy is particularly useful in dealing with these situations because it places rhetorical statements in the context of the information (backup) cited, thereby allowing unsupported inferences and unjustified conclusions to be tested.

Developing Cognitive Skills with MECA/SM Strategy

MECA/SM analyses are presented graphically as illustrations or cognitive diagrams. As you have seen earlier in this chapter, the parts that make up one of these diagrams are labeled *Purpose*, *Resources*, *Activities*, and *Consequences*. Interpretations or discussions typically proceed in that order. When used in that sequence, a MECA/SM analysis represents a logical sequence of beginning, middle, and end, and as such it can be readily understood. This standard sequence itself as a basis for critically engaging subject matter is neither necessarily nor overtly critical; being ideologically and semantically neutral, it allows for the employment of all those cognitive skills associated with critical thinking that are necessary to yet higher-order thinking.

The act of reviewing a completed MECA/SM analysis, one developed by another, provides the reviewer with the basis for critically engaging both the subject matter and the analyst's grasp of the subject matter.

The act of evaluating MECA/SM analysis is more overtly critical, and it promotes the higher-order thinking skills associated with understanding, analysis, and evaluation.

The act of developing one's own original MECA/SM analysis yields an effective framework for discussing subject matter at various cognitive levels and from a variety of viewpoints.

The cognitive skills associated with critical thinking have been categorized in many ways by many researchers and writers. If one takes a general description of critical thinking as being the questioning or inquiry that we engage in when seeking to understand, evaluate, or resolve; and if one adds to that description the taxonomic and process-oriented descriptions of critical thinking (discussed in chapter 1), then one may summarize the categories of cognitive skills as follows:

- understanding skills

- analysis and evaluation skills

- problem-solving skills

To these may be added a fourth set of skills, which in a meaningful way spring from close involvement with the first three:

- creative skills

Using Paul's (1990) descriptors for cognitive skills, the following list of cognitive actions shows the basic MECA/SM approach as correlated with cognitive skills. [The bracketed statements show the use of each descriptor in MECA/SM].

Understanding Skills

MECA/SM helps one do the following:

- *clarify words and phrases* [Words and phrases are made to take their dynamic position in the means-ends transformation.]

- *note similarities and differences* [Static and dynamic means are distinguished, allowing differentiation among groups of resources and activities.]

- *distinguish the important from the trivial* [What is relevant to the means-ends transformation is extracted.]

- *see contradictions* [Discern when means do not support the purpose(s); when result does not follow from stated purpose.]

- *explore implications* [Determine consequences.]

- *provide a basis for evaluating evidence and alleged facts* [Facts can be verified by determining and evaluating the means that produced them.] *

- *understand arguments, interpretations, theories, actions, and policies.* [The act of means-ends transformation requires analysis, comparison, and exploration.]

An important aspect of means-ends strategy is that it establishes an informed foundation for further exploration and for engaging in dialogical and dialectical questioning. Dialogical questioning refers to exploring subject matter until a thorough understanding is achieved. Dialectical questioning refers to defending or opposing a particular point of view once existing views have been explored and understood.

Analysis and Evaluation and the Development of Cognitive Skills

MECA/SM representations are usually designed in this order: *Purpose, Resources, Activities, Consequences.* This order or pattern and the attendant analytical and evaluative cognitive processes that it engenders, run as follows:

---

* For example, if a statement of purpose is assumed to be a statement of fact, as in: "One purpose of blood is to rid the body of waste material," then the means cited become the basis for establishing the fact, and the consequences become the basis for evaluating the fidelity of associated inferences that may follow.

- *develop confidence in reasoning abilities* [Analysts gain the ability to see the means-ends dynamic inherent in all subject matter and situations.]

- *develop independent thought* [New subject matter can be approached from a means-ends perspective.]

- *develop fair-mindedness by becoming sensitive to egocentric and sociocentric thought* [Means-ends analysis provides a clear basis for evaluating whether a presentation or viewpoint is one-sided.]

- *suspend judgment yet persevere tenaciously in thought* [The nature of means-ends transformations requires that the analysis be complete before evaluations can be made. Given its graphical nature, any areas that have not been addressed in a MECA/SM analysis are made readily apparent.]

Paul's descriptors apply to those cognitive skills that must be possessed by a person to be thoughtful and reflective, analytical and evaluative. By using the questions associated with the means-ends taxonomy that appear in the next chapter, one can see how these cognitive skills are developed within the MECA/SM framework.

Problem-solving Skills

A close relationship prevails between the *Activities* portion of a MECA/SM analysis and systematic problem-solving. If the material under analysis has a history of including particular problem-solving sequences, or can be interpreted as such, then these sequences can be portrayed in the *Activities* portion of a MECA/SM analysis. Alternatively, the MECA/SM framework can itself serve as a problem-solving scheme. In these cases, the *Purpose* becomes a statement of the problem to be solved, the means (*Resources, Activities*) becomes the basis for identifying solutions, and the *Consequences* serves to identify the likely results of solving the problem.

Creative-thinking Skills

Several approaches exist for developing creative-thinking skills, and they are documented in the works of Guilford, Osborn, Parnes, and others. Means-ends analysis represents another aid to creative thinking. A standard means-ends analysis, because it results in a new representation of subject matter, is an inherently creative operation in the sense that it synthesizes information and ideas in a manner not previously conceived. Creative thinking is fostered also because means-ends strategy requires the analyst to ponder consequences and in this manner produce ideas that may have gone previously undiscovered.

A teacher can use a partial MECA/SM diagram to prompt creative thinking in the students. By supplying an essentially blank model (with perhaps just a few resources, or a few processes, or an incomplete statement of purpose or consequences), analysts can be asked to complete the analysis in any way they see fit. This "blank" approach frees both the teacher and the student from traditional restraints, and it allows their imaginations to suggest a variety of creative interpretations. (See Chapter 8 for a discussion of using this approach in your classroom.)

MECA/SM methodology involves the analysis of raw subject matter to reveal purposes, resources, activities, and consequences. These elements are natural and inherent in all subject matter. Identifying, representing, and evaluating the dynamic relationships that these elements bear to one another provides the opportunity to develop those cognitive skills associated with understanding, analysis, evaluation, problem-solving, and creativity. In sum, MECA/SM strategy provides an effective framework for discussing subject matter while simultaneously developing those cognitive skills that a person needs to do critical thinking.

MECA/SM methodology involves the analysis of raw subject matter to reveal purposes, resources, activities, and consequences. These elements are natural and inherent in all subject matter.

6 Fundamentals of MECA/SM Methodology

All subject matter serves some end-in-view or purpose. An end-in-view is achieved through the use of necessary means. Achieving the end-in-view by way of necessary means leads to consequences. Consequences can be either positive or negative, or both positive and negative.

Because all subject matter serves some purpose, all subject matter is capable of being analyzed through a means-ends strategy. Means-Ends Critical Analysis of Subject Matter (MECA/SM) methodology involves the analysis of subject matter to reveal the purposes, resources, activities, and consequences (results or effects) that are inherent in that subject matter.

MECA/SM analyses are developed and presented in a diagrammatic format that might be called a cognitive visualization. The parts of the diagram are labeled *Purpose, Resources, Activities,* and *Consequences,* and analyses are usually developed in this P-R-A-C sequence.

The logic of the MECA/SM approach to subject matter is set forth in the following chart:

The Framework for MECA/SM

The Logic of
Means-Ends Critical Analysis of Subject Matter

1. Means ————> End-in-view ————> Consequences

OR

2. Static Means + Dynamic Means –>End-in-view –> Consequences

OR

3. Resources + Activities ————> Purpose ————> Results

Although "Purpose" appears "in the middle" of the three sequences, it is logically, and usually, the first element that is thought of and identified by the teacher or student when performing a MECA/SM analysis. Note that although "M" (for means) appears first in the acronym MECA/SM, it is actually the "E" (for "ends" or "purpose") that is thought of and identified first by the analyst.

One can, of course, begin a means-ends consequential analysis anywhere in the process: One can begin at the end, and reason backwards through means and causes to purposes and intentions; one can begin in the middle; one can begin at the beginning. One good service that the MECA/SM format performs for the analyst, in any event, is to structure a logical and consequential picture of the whole process, once all of its parts have been properly identified and diagrammatically distributed. To facilitate recording, understanding, and visualizing of the subject matter under analysis, use of the following diagrammatic templates is recommended. I myself prefer Style 1; nonetheless, depending on where one begins the process and the approach one takes, any one of the styles works just fine.

Sample MECA/SM Diagrams: How to Do It

Let's assume that a person plays tennis to keep fit through exercise. Physical fitness through tennis is the person's end-in-view or purpose. The necessary means used to achieve that end in that way include the static means: a tennis court, tennis equipment, and another

One can, of course, begin a MECA/SM analysis anywhere in the process.

player; and the dynamic means, the actual playing of the game—serving, volleying, returning, and keeping score. One positive consequence of playing tennis includes good body tone and increased stamina. One negative consequence may be a skinned knee or twisted ankle. One negative consequence of not engagning in a regimen of physical fitness, whether through playing tennis or through some other means, is that one may become a couch-potato.

The following diagram shows a MECA/SM analysis of the game of tennis. Note that the activities (the dynamic means) imply the use of the resources (the static means). Also note that each of the four components within the analysis are numbered to suggest the usual order of development.

Title: MECA/SM Analysis of Tennis

1) PURPOSE (Why?)

to keep fit through playing tennis

2) RESOURCES (What is used?)

- players
- court
- ball
- racquets

3) ACTIVITIES (What is done?)

- serve
- volley
- return
- keep score

4) CONSEQUENCES (What can happen if purpose is achieved?)

- POSITIVE

- good body tone and increased stamina

- NEGATIVE

- possible skinned knee or twisted ankle

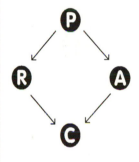

Fundamentals of MECA/SM Methodology

The four elements in a MECA/SM analysis are *Purpose, Resources, Activities,* and *Consequences.* The following illustration describes the type of entries that can accompany each of the four elements.

Title: The Structural Elements in MECA/SM Analysis

1) PURPOSE (Why?)
a purpose is any end-in-view

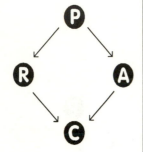

2) RESOURCES (What is needed?)
Resources fall into any one or more of these categories:

- human
- social
- institutional
- economic
- elemental

3) ACTIVITIES (What is done?)
Activities can be one or more of the following:

- natural
- mental
- physical
- technological

4) CONSEQUENCES (What can happen if purpose is achieved?)
- POSITIVE
- NEGATIVE

A consequence or effect is the likely result or outcome of achieving the purpose.

Both positive and negative results of achieving the purpose are considered. One may also consider the positive and negative consequences of not achieving the purpose.

Although one may begin anywhere in the process and reason to all the parts, when fully stated, an analysis develops first by identifying the purpose served by the subject matter under analysis, then by identifying necessary resources needed to achieve the purpose, next by identifying the activities that will put the resources to use, and finally by considering the consequences (results, effects) of achieving the purpose.

Purpose is stated as one or more ends-in-view. Statements of purpose can be narrow and information-based, such as in stating that the purpose of the formula c =2(pi)r is "to calculate a circle's circumference"; or they may be broad and therefore subject to wide interpretation, as in stating that the purpose of war is "to restore peace." In any event, statements of purpose make sense best when they start with the word "to," so that one's thoughts can be sharply focused.

Resources necessary to achieve the purpose are identified next. Resources can be human (a biologist, an educator, a doctor, an engineer, or anyone else), social (families, communities, organizations), institutional (a college, a religious organization, a government agency), economic (capital, interest rates, monetary policy), or elemental (earth, wind, fire, water, or the things composed of the elements).

Activities that employ the resources are considered next. Activities are natural (e.g. letting a garden grow), mental (e.g. the steps used to calculate an arithmetic value), physical (e.g. the steps involved in building a house), or technological (e.g. the robotic assembly of automobiles). Sometimes the various processes become almost indistinguishable, such as when a writer uses a keyboard (physical) to compose a document (mental) with the aid of a computerized word processor (technological) that is plugged into an outlet to obtain electricity produced with the aid of a waterfall (natural).

Consequences represent the likely results (aftereffects) of actually achieving the end-in-view. Consequences can be positive or negative. An analyst may also consider the consequences of not achieving the stated purpose.

MECA/SM
on
MECA/SM

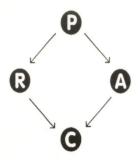

As another example, here is an overview of MECA/SM methodology summarizing the framework of means-ends critical analysis of subject matter itself. In this overview, I use MECA/SM strategy to analyze MECA/SM itself and to explore implications for thinking, teaching, and learning.

Title: MECA/SM Analysis of MECA/SM

1) PURPOSE
to analyze the analysis of subject matter

2) RESOURCES (What is needed?)
- experience
- written, spoken, or viewed material
- imagination
- analyst

3) ACTIVITIES (What is done?)
- establish title for the analysis
- determine the purpose of the subject matter at hand
- identify and arrange the subject-matter resources
- identify and arrange the subject-matter processes or activities
- determine the consequences (positive and negative)
- evaluate the analysis for internal consistency and fair-mindedness

4) CONSEQUENCES (What can happen if purpose is achieved?)
- POSITIVE

Regarding subject matter:
- a diagrammatic view of the dynamic and critical relationships inherent in the subject matter
- a basis for establishing similar views for related subject-matter topics

Regarding teachers:
- a means for critically analyzing subject matter
- a means to deliver subject matter and simultaneously to develop students' critical-thinking skills
- a means to assess achievement critically

Regarding students:

- a means for critically analyzing subject matter
- the development of a critical understanding of subject matter
- the development of cognitive skills

  - NEGATIVE

Regarding subject matter:

- If the analysis is poorly made, a critical view of the subject matter will not be obtained.

Regarding teachers:

- If the strategy is poorly understood, its use will not develop a critical understanding of subject matter. The strategy will not be effective for critical delivery and assessment, and it will not develop students' critical-thinking skills.

Regarding students:

- If the strategy is poorly understood, its use will not develop a critical understanding of subject matter. The strategy will not lead to a critical understanding of subject matter and the development of cognitive skills.

Carrying MECA/SM to an Nth Degree

The entries in an analysis may be subdivided or subordinated to any extent necessary to promote both clarity and completeness. As a practical matter of classroom discussion and readability, analyses that go beyond the second degree of division should be avoided because they tend to become too dense, too busy, thus obscuring the main points made in the analysis. Analyses may, however, be constructed to any degree desired. In fact, some of the *Resources* in the illustration on pp. 74-75 are carried to a third degree of division (denoted by the ■ marks), and elements of the *Activities* and *Consequences* are carried to a second degree (denoted by ◆ marks).

In addition to showing how the entries in an analysis can be subdivided to promote clarity, understanding, and comprehensiveness, note the following in the illustration on pp. 74-75:

1. A full analysis includes the analyst's name, the general subject matter, a specific topic within that subject matter, and space to identify the source of the material under analysis.

2. The word "raw" in the phrase "Source of raw material" permanently makes the point that all material remains raw to the analyst until it has been critically reconstructed through use of some cognitive strategy.

3. The source of the material under analysis may refer either to one's own experience or to a book or other source of information. If the analysis is based on one's experience, then the term "experience" is entered. If based on something read, viewed, heard, or observed, then as complete a reference as possible is entered so that a reader of the analysis may check the analyst's sources.

4. The asterisks (*) signify entries that do not appear in the raw material but which the analyst added because they either were implied in the discussion, they allowed a more even flow of ideas, or, as in the case of *Consequences* the nature of MECA/SM prompted, helped, and allowed them to be discovered as likely aftereffects.

5. When reviewing any MECA/SM analysis, bear in mind the metacognitive aspects of thinking *with* MECA/SM. In other words, as you look at the topics and their place in the analysis, be aware that you are reviewing them within a cognitively critical framework. At least two things are taking place: You are learning about the subject matter, and your learning is taking place within a framework of critical reflection. The subject matter is not only being learned but

also it is being thought about critically. Stated another way, be consciously and continually aware of the cognitive strategies that underlie your thought processes about the subject matter.

6. When starting to read an analysis, take the last part of its title and the statement of purpose together. Turn the page to see the example. The title "MECA/SM Analysis of Human Nutrition" and the purposeful statement "to maintain a healthy body" are combined to read as follows: "The purpose of human nutrition is to maintain a healthy body." See another example on p. 76: The title "MECA/SM Analysis of the Human Digestive System" and the purposeful statement "to extract nutrients from food" are combined to read: "The purpose of the human digestive system is to extract nutrients from food."

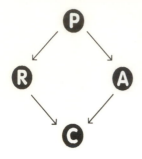

Analyst: Theresa DeCaro, student, Queensborough
    Community College
Subject: Science   *Topic*: Biology
Source of raw material: Textbook: W.D. Schraer and
    H.J. Stoltze, *A Comprehensive Text for New York
    State* (Newton, M.: A&B, Inc., 1986): Chapter 15,
    "H.N."

Title: MECA/SM Analysis
of Human Nutrition

1) PURPOSE (Why?)

to maintain a healthy body

2) RESOURCES (What is needed?)

- brain
- hunger
- food
  - ◆ roughage
    - ▪ fruits
    - ▪ vegetables
    - ▪ grains
  - ◆ nutrients
    - ▪ carbohydrates
      - ▲ sugar
      - ▲ starches
    - ▪ lipids
      - ▲ oils
      - ▲ fats
    - ▪ proteins
    - ▪ water
    - ▪ vitamins
    - ▪ minerals
    - ▪ food additives
  - ◆ calories
- digestive system

3) ACTIVITIES (What is done?)

- feel hungry
- eat food
- digest food
- drink water
- include roughage in diet
  - ◆ keeps food moving in
    esophagus
  - ◆ aids elimination of waste
- give the body rest
- exercise the body
- seek medical advice

4) CONSEQUENCES (What can happen if purpose is achieved?)

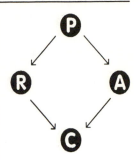

• POSITIVE
  ◆ healthful foods are eaten
  ◆ the correct amount of food is eaten
  ◆ there are fewer medical problems
  ◆ better mental capabilities are attained
  ◆ a more active lifestyle is achieved
  ◆ a longer life span can be expected

• NEGATIVE
  ◆ unhealthful foods are eaten
  ◆ incorrect amount of foods eaten
    ▪ eating disorders develop
    ▪ obesity
    ▪ anorexia nervosa
  ◆ disorders of the large intestine develop
  ◆ deficiency diseases occur
  ◆ stomach ulcers develop
  ◆ a shorter life span can be expected

The foregoing sample analysis represents an overview of material in one chapter in a biology textbook. MECA/SM is extremely helpful in gaining this sort of visual overview in a timely, broad, and critical manner. An overview like this can be generated for any textbook chapter or material. One often wishes, however, to delve deeper into subject matter, to follow an analytical pathway.

For example, if one wanted to understand more concerning "digest food" or "include roughage in diet" or any of the *Resources* such as proteins, minerals, food additives; or any other element in the analysis, one could reenter the chapter, locate the discussion on the topic of interest, and perform a MECA/SM analysis on that topic specifically.

Let's suppose that the analyst wanted further to explore the topic "digestive system." Here is an analysis of that topic using material from the same chapter:

Waves, Pathways, and Styles

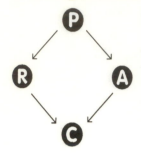

Title: MECA/SM Analysis of the Human Digestive System

1) PURPOSE (Why?)
to extract nutrients from food

2) RESOURCES (What is needed?)
- food passage
  - oral cavity (mouth)
  - pharynx (throat)
  - esophagus (gullet)
  - stomach
  - small intestine
  - large intestine
  - rectum
  - anus
- accessory organs
  - salivary glands
  - liver
  - gall bladder
  - pancreas

3) ACTIVITIES (What is done?)
- food enters body through mouth
- food is passed to stomach
- food is mixed with gastric juices
- food is broken down (and nutrients extracted) in small intestine
- undigested food passes into large intestine
- large intestine
  - reabsorbs water
  - absorbs vitamins
  - eliminates undigested/ undigestible material

4) CONSEQUENCES (What can happen if purpose is achieved?)
- POSITIVE

body uses nutrients to maintain itself

- NEGATIVE

absence of nutrients can lead to body breakdown

Having made the preceding analysis, the analyst may now wish to understand more concerning the absorption of vitamins in the large intestines. Still using the same chapter as raw material, here is that analysis:

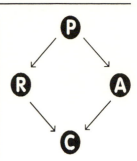

Title: MECA/SM Analysis of the Large Intestine

1) PURPOSE (Why?)

to absorb vitamin K and water

2) RESOURCES (What is needed?)

- large intestine
- undigested food material
- large intestine bacteria
- water

3) ACTIVITIES (What is done?)

- bacteria feed on undigested food material
- bacteria produce vitamins K and B
- vitamins are absorbed with water

4) CONSEQUENCES (What can happen if purpose is achieved?)

- POSITIVE

blood can clot

- NEGATIVE

blood will not clot

The three foregoing analyses, all based on the same chapter in the biology text, constitute an *analytical pathway*. An analytical pathway is determined by the analyst's need or desire to develop a more thorough, more detailed, understanding of subject matter. In the present case, the initial analysis provided an overall introduction to the topic of human nutrition, which led to an analysis of the digestive system, which prompted an analysis of the absorption of vitamins. These pathways, or nested analyses, allow an analyst to pursue an area of interest in a manner that develops a thorough and critical understanding of the topic at hand. In this example, the pathway can be further traveled either by picking any topic from the third analysis, perhaps blood clotting, or the analyst may return to any of the analyses, select another *Resource* or *Activity*, and enter a new pathway.

Wonderful things can happen to us while traveling analytical pathways! The book, chapter, or material that opened the gate to the initial pathway may not contain enough information on a topic. To continue on the path, one may have to use other sources of information. We may have to read more books, talk to people, ask questions, seek new resources. These are the activities and experiences that help develop the cognitive skills of understanding, analysis, evaluation, and problem-solving. These are the skills we use in school, in the university, in the workplace, and all our lives long.

Which topics ought one to select and how far ought one to travel along a pathway? The answer lies in your response to these questions: How important is the topic to you? How much interest does the topic hold for you? How intellectually uncomfortable will you feel if you fail to achieve a comprehensive understanding of the topic?

Cognitive Waves

An analytical pathway allows an analyst to stay on the trail of a given topic, to follow a topic until its essence has been discovered. A *cognitive wave* allows an analyst to set out on a totally different topic.

Unlike pathways whose points of departure are taken primarily from existing *Resources* and *Activities*, cognitive waves emanate primarily from entries associated with *Consequences*. A cognitive wave is started by turning a statement of result into a new statement of purpose. Here are some examples with respect to the "MECA/SM Analysis of Human Nutrition." The result "the right foods are eaten" is reformulated purposively as "to eat the right foods"; "the correct amount of foods are eaten" is reformulated with purpose and intent as "to eat the correct amount of food"; and "better mental capabilities are attained" gets new aim as "to attain better mental capabilities."

The analyses that ensue from these statements of purpose ("to") will flow out from the topic originally considered, enticing the analyst to venture into fields far beyond the initial point of departure. Riding cognitive waves, taken at their height, leads on to interdisciplinary, interconnected, intellectual adventure and a critical view of the world.

Cognitive Diagram Styles

Just as one may begin a MECA/SM analyses at any point in the process, so also MECA/SM analyses can be diagrammed in a variety of ways. The following templates show this variety:

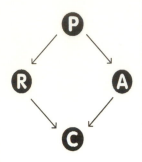

STYLE 1

The advantage of Style 1's arrangement is that emphasis falls on *Purpose* as the initial focus of one's analysis. In this approach, one groups the means *(Resources* and *Activities)* horizontally on the page. This is the format that I prefer and use throughout this book.

Analyst:
Subject: *Topic*:
Source of raw material:

Title: MECA/SM Analysis of

_____

1) PURPOSE (Why?)

2) RESOURCES (What is needed?)   3) ACTIVITIES (What is done?)

•

•

•

•

4) CONSEQUENCES (What can happen if purpose is achieved?)

• POSITIVE

• NEGATIVE

STYLE 2

In the Style 2 arrangement, *Purpose* is placed *after* the means; the implication is that a purpose is something to be anticipated and achieved and is therefore "off in the distance" (the right side of the page). Once completed, the sequence of *Resources-Activities-Purpose* appears as a logical start-to-end analysis. In practice, I have found that although the four elements are numbered as to their normal order of consideration, some analysts find the arrangement confusing when they use a style that does not start with *Purpose* first.

Analyst:
Subject: *Topic*:
Source of raw material:

Title: MECA/SM Analysis of

_____

2) RESOURCES   **3) ACTIVITIES**   **1) PURPOSE**
(What is needed?)   (What is done?)   (Why?)

•   •   •

•   •

4) CONSEQUENCES (What can happen if purpose is achieved?)

• POSITIVE

• NEGATIVE

STYLE 3

The Style 3 arrangement was invented by a student. When I asked why he used this arrangement, he answered: "This way, I can start to think about the consequences of something I might have in mind." The idea of thinking about the implications of some intended action (some purpose) before the action is taken, can be most powerful. It causes the analyst to think of the likely results, both positive and negative, of doing something before that something is done. Style 3 certainly promotes this forethought, but full consideration of consequences (results) cannot be effectively made until the accompanying resources and activities have been identified and understood.

Analyst:
Subject: *Topic*:
Source of raw material:

Title: MECA/SM Analysis of

_____

1) PURPOSE (Why?)

4) CONSEQUENCES (What can happen if purpose is achieved?):
- POSITIVE

- NEGATIVE

2) RESOURCES (What is needed?)   3) ACTIVITIES (What is done?)
-
                                          -

-
                                          -

STYLE 4

While Style 4 deemphasizes the diagrammatic nature of MECA/SM, it does simplify writing up and typing an analysis.

Analyst:

Subject:　　　　　　　　*Topic*:

Source of raw material:

Title: MECA/SM Analysis of

_____

1) PURPOSE (Why?)

2) RESOURCES (What is needed?)

●

●

3) ACTIVITIES (What is done?)

●

●

(4) CONSEQUENCES (What can happen if purpose is achieved?)
  ● POSITIVE

  ● NEGATIVE

Even when styles of diagrams are used other than the logical sequence of Style 1, the analyst must maintain the 1-2-3-4 numbering of the elements of the diagram in order to keep the sequence of logic in view.

It is far less important to appreciate the different styles possible for MECA/SM analysis diagram than it is to develop the logical discipline to proceed through an analysis in the sequential order *Purpose-Resources-Activities-Consequences*. This point holds true for any diagrammatic rearrangements that you may develop.

A Taxonomic View of MECA/SM

As in the case of taxonomies devised by Bloom, Paul, and others, the following MECA/SM taxonomy may be used to evaluate the development of cognitive skills. Notice that the evaluation questions may be asked, and in many instances *answered*, by *either* the teacher *or* the student. This taxonomy shows the thorough and practical self-assessing features that are inherent in MECA/SM analyses.

Information-based and rhetoric-based means-ends analyses alike can be evaluated with the assistance of this means-ends taxonomy.

MECA/SM evaluations are conducted with two concerns in mind: internal consistency and fair-mindedness. An evaluation for internal consistency is about making sure that the analysis is true to the MECA/SM framework. This means making sure that the analysis is about the purpose of the subject matter, is supported by means, and that positive and negative results are shown. An evaluation for fair-mindedness is concerned with determining whether the analysis (and therefore, the material analyzed), is free of bias, prejudice, and misrepresentation.

The questions in each section achieve their greatest evaluative effect when they are asked both *during* the reconstruction of the information into knowledge, and *after* the reconstruction into a MECA/SM cognitive diagram has been effected. The taxonomy is presented in the order that a means-analysis is normally conducted: *Purpose, Resources, Activities, Consequences.*

Internal consistency refers to the faithfulness of the representation to the means-ends framework. In performing an evaluation for internal consistency, one tries not to impose an external or personal viewpoint but rather to see if the analysis is structurally sound in that the stated means adequately support the intended purpose, and the consequences logically follow from the purpose. Once this has been established, an evaluation for fair-mindedness may follow.

Evaluating for fair-mindedness (against bias, prejudice, or misrepresentation) involves making sure that a means-ends analyst does not either intentionally or unintentionally represent unfairly another idea, group, issue, theory, belief, or any viewpoint that is likely to be subject to multiple interpretations.

The following taxonomy, parallel to a MECA/SM analysis, has five main parts: *Title, Purpose, Resources, Activities,* and *Consequences.* Each part has two taxonomic subdivisions: "Evaluating for Internal Consistency" and "Evaluating for Fair-mindedness."

Evaluating a Title for Internal Consistency

T1: Does the analysis have a title?
A title indicates the topic addressed by the analysis. Without a title, the analyst (and the reader of the analysis) has no initial analytical direction.

T2: Does the title address two or more topics?
Titles that address more than one topic will probably require a dual set of purposes, resources, activities, and consequences. This can lead to a completed analysis that can be difficult to understand. Topics may be broad or

narrow, it is best to restrict the analysis to only one specific topic per title.

Evaluating a Title for Fair-mindedness

T3: Is the title overtly biased?

If an analyst can support a position in a fair-minded way, then it is all right to takes sides, but the title, "A MECA/SM Analysis of Why Socialism Has Failed," for example, contains an *a priori* embedded negative judgment, and it holds the potential for making the subsequent analysis one-sided. The reader of such analyses must be alert to the potential for propagandizing.

T4: Does the title include a consequence?

A title that says that something has "failed" (to continue the example) or is "good" or is "not good," indicates that the analyst has (a) made a broad and as yet unsupported statement, and (b) identified a consequence. For whom has it failed? Under what conditions? With what means? The ensuing analysis itself should support the conclusions, and such conclusions–either positive or negative–should properly appear in the *Consequences* portion of the analysis.

Evaluating Purpose for Internal Consistency

P1: Is the statement of purpose connected logically to the title?

If a title includes a reference to some idea, and that idea is not reflected in the statement of purpose, then you will have uncovered an anomaly. At this point, one can expect that when the analysis is completed, the title may need to be changed, or perhaps the stated purpose may need to be restated.

P2: Is a statement of purpose present?

Evaluations of MECA/SM analyses must include a statement of purpose because, without a clear statement of purpose, it is difficult to determine whether the remainder of the analysis is appropriate.

P3: Is the statement actually a declaration of purpose?

Depending on the analyst's degree of sophistication with MECA/SM strategy, statements of purpose may be erroneously described as a resource, an activity, or (and this is more likely) a consequence. See P12. If the statement starts with the word "to," it is likely to be a statement of purpose.

P4: Is the purpose drawn from within the subject matter itself, rather than being merely about the subject matter?

This is an area that tends to confuse teacher and student alike. The reliance on learning objectives has so distorted and minimized the true nature of subject matter that confusion regarding statements that are about the subject matter, on the one hand, and those that come from within the subject matter, on the other hand, are often confused. (See Chapter 3 for further discussion.)

P5: Is the stated purpose appropriate to the cited means?

Purposes unsupported by appropriate means (resources and activities) will not be achieved, and anticipated consequences will not follow.

P6: Does the purpose include its own means or consequences?

See P10 and P15.

P7: If two or more purposes are stated, are they related?

Sometimes analyses will contain two or more related purposes. If the purposes are closely related, then the means cited and consequences anticipated are likely to be supportive.

P8: Are there two or more unrelated purposes at play?

If the two or more purposes are widely different, then an equal number of sets of means and results must appear in the analysis. In such cases, it is good to make separate MECA/SM analyses for each purpose.

P9: Are separate purposes supported by separate means?

Although it is possible for one analysis to depict separate purposes, the analyst must group, but not intermingle, the related means and results. Again, to avoid analyses that have so many entries that understanding is made difficult, it is best to provide separate diagrams. Just what constitutes "too many entries" will depend on the topic being analyzed, the difficulty level of the material, and good judgment, gained through experience, of what constitutes a readily understood analysis.

P10: Given the means, might the stated purpose actually be a consequence?

To avoid confusing a result with a purpose, one may ask this question: Does the result follow the purpose in *logic* and in *time*? In the example of the analysis of blood, if the purposes and results were switched, then we are faced with a logical inconsistency. If the purpose were to maintain and repair body tissue, then that could not lead to a result that delivers oxygen to body tissue and that rids the body of waste material. In this case, although the sequence may be logically switched, it would not be possible to maintain and repair body tissue without its *first* being supplied with oxygen and other nutrients, so the *time sequence* test is not met. If one wanted, as a purpose, "to show how body tissue is maintained and repaired," that would be a decidedly different means-ends analysis involving a description of the mechanism whereby blood picks up and delivers nutrients to body tissue.

Evaluating Purpose for Fair-mindedness

P11: Given the means, is the purpose misstated or misrepresented?

Unlike P7, this is not so much a logical test as it is a test twisting or distorting facts to make a point that would otherwise be unsupportable.

P12: Does the stated purpose misrepresent or put another idea, group, or viewpoint at an unfair disadvantage?

If a third party attributes motives (purposes) to another group or individual, the possibility for distortion is always present. If A tells B that C's purpose in attending a meeting is to put B in a bad light, and if B believes A uncritically and does not discuss the matter directly with C, then B is at the mercy of A's interpretation of events. In other words, get both (or all) sides of a story before making your own judgment. In terms of means-ends analysis, we have to look for resources, activities, and consequences (statements, actions, interpretations) that represent the other sides.

P13: Is there an implied purpose?

Implied purposes are those that do not appear as actual statements in the analyzed passage but are situationally inherent. For example, a politician makes a speech, the stated purpose of which is to show how bad things have become under an incumbent's leadership, but whose unstated or implied purpose is to cause the speaker to become the new leader.

P14: Is there a suggestion or possibility of a hidden purpose?

Hidden purposes can be quite difficult to uncover. In situations concerning political speeches, to continue the example, one is usually prepared to appreciate that implied purposes are often afoot, but not when speeches or written materials are less evidently in the vested interests of their authors. Public officials may support a change in zoning for certain real-estate tracts, for example, declaring that they have no interest in the decision one way or another, but then it later comes to light that the brother of an official's spouse plans to develop a regional shopping center on the tracts in question. That is what I mean when I say that hidden purposes are sometimes hard to spy.

P15: Are other purposes that might be at odds with the stated or implied purpose fairly represented?

This is a variation of P13, but it has more to do with comprehensiveness than with intended or unintended distortion. Because a single problem may have several possible solutions, one must keep an open mind to allow for all valid possibilities. If in the context of problem-solving a statement of purpose is too narrow, then it may presuppose a solution and hence the necessary means and results. For example, there are several ways to transport people between two points, but if the statement of purpose reads "to transport people from point A to point B via bus," then the means (bus) to the solution has been built into the statement of purpose. In such instances, other solutions are not likely to be considered.

P16: Are there alternative ways of conceptualizing the end-in-view that would lead to alternative means and results?

Consider these two statements of purpose:

"to provide health insurance for all citizens"

"to provide health care for all citizens"

The first purpose might lead to a system that required privately funded health care (individuals would choose their own doctor), while the second might lead to a public, tax-funded health-care program (area clinics).

Evaluating Resources for Internal Consistency

Evaluating resources requires accounting for the indicated resources necessary to achieving the purpose.

R1: Are resources present in the analysis?

This is a simple check for completeness to determine whether resources are present in the analysis.

R2: Have all appropriate human resources been accounted for?

Are those people necessary to achieving the purpose represented?

R3: Have all appropriate social resources been accounted for?

Are all necessary community groups, companies, corporations, and other organizations represented?

R4: Have all appropriate institutional resources been accounted for?

Are all necessary school, religious, and government agencies represented?

R5: Have all appropriate economic resources, been accounted for?

Are all necessary land, labor, capital, and other economic factors represented?

R6: Have all appropriate basic resources been accounted for?

Are all necessary natural resources and the possibility of natural occurrences represented?

R7: Are other necessary resources accounted for?

What other resources exist that might likely be useful to achieve the purpose represented?

R8: Are the stated resources appropriate to the purpose?

Can the identified resources potentially be used to achieve the purposes they are capable of, and can they actually be used to achieve the stated purposes?

Evaluating Resources for Fair-mindedness

R9: Are the resources stated factual?

Are the resources represented as actual figures, events, and true statements?

R10: Are the resources properly represented ?

Have those resources represented by figures, events, and statements been accurately portrayed?

R11: Are the resources timely?

Are the cited facts the very latest information available so that what was true at one time can be taken as being true now?

R12: Are inferences correctly drawn?

Are any entries that are not actually factual, but are based on fact, logically drawn? Are these derivative entries identified as such? In the example, on pp. 53-54, a dairymaid is cited as a resource. Let us assume that the writer of the passage about immunization did not know for sure whether the donor of the "matter" were actually a dairymaid. It might appear reasonable to suggest that the donor had been a dairymaid because Dr. Jenner worked with dairy cows, and these animals were often attended by dairymaids. This being the case, the careful and precise analyst would parenthetically identify all inferred resources as such: "dairymaid (inferred)."

Evaluating Activities for Internal Consistency

A1: Are activities present in the analysis?

This is a check for completeness to determine whether activities are present in the analysis.

A2: Are the stated activities appropriate to the purpose?

Some activities may actually have no relation to the stated purpose. In this instance, either the activities have been incorrectly identified or one may be working with an implied but unstated purpose or both.

A3: Have all necessary activities been identified?

All activities required to achieve the purpose must be identified in the analysis. In some instances, the analyst may leave it to the reader of the analysis to infer some activity. In that case, it is preferable to show the activities in writing.

A4: Are related activities grouped?

Activities that are related should be grouped together.

*A5: Do grouped activities represent a coherent se-
    quence?*

Activities that are thought to be related must represent a coherent start-to-finish sequence or, at a minimum,
should represent a logical sequence.

A6: Do there appear to be too many entries?

Sometimes the processes described are so complex
that too many activities are listed, and this inhibits understanding. If the processes being described become over-
long, this is a hint that there may be more than one
purpose at play. See P8.

*A7: Do the activities account for the use of all re-
    sources?*

Taken as a whole, do all the activities in one way or
another employ all the resources, either directly or indirectly.

Evaluating Activities for Fair-mindedness

*A8: Do the activities rely on resources not present in
    the analysis?*

In trying to show that some purpose is attainable
through the stated activities, the unfairminded analyst may
intentionally leave out necessary resources. These resources may not be attainable, available, or appropriate,
and so the analyst may unfairly seek to hide them.

*A9: Is the process slanted to produce the stated pur-
    pose?*

Do any activities, present or missing, give the impression that something is possible when actually it is not
generally accepted as reasonable? In the example of the
passage on immunization, if the second inoculation activity were not actually performed, then that would make the
purpose unachievable.

*A10: Are there alternative activities that could serve
    the same purpose?*

Purposes often lend themselves to more than one set
of means. In the inoculation example, the stated purpose in

the passage is to protect the boy from disease. If this were actually the case, why then was the boy subjected to an experimental procedure in the first place? Dr. Jenner had a different implicit purpose in mind when he inoculated the boy, namely, to find a vaccine that could be generally applied. If the purpose had been to protect that particular boy, then injecting him with the "matter" would not have been one of the activities; rather, activities that served to remove the boy from harm would have been appropriate to the stated purpose. In other words, the means employed may cover hidden motives.

A11: Are the activities shown ethically/morally justified?

Do the ends justify the means? (If the ends do not justify the means, then what does?) This is a question one must ask when evaluating activities for fair-mindedness in situations that are dangerous, volatile, or unpredictable. In the case of the immunization, one may question Dr. Jenner's ethics in exposing a human being to a life-threatening situation. Was the boy warned in advance of the consequences? Were the consequences played down to gain his cooperation in the experiment? In either case, and given his age, the boy could not be expected to defend his own interests.

A12: Are unnecessary activities included?

Are the activities unnecessary to achieve the purpose but included to serve some vested interest? In the case of changing the zoning for a tract of real estate, title to the land may be clear and unquestioned, but a title search may be ordered anyway to serve the economic interests of concerned parties.

Evaluating Consequences for Internal Consistency

C1: Are the likely aftereffects of achieving the purpose identified?

This is a simple check for completeness to determine whether foreseeable results have been considered and are present in the analysis.

C2: Do the stated consequences follow from the stated purpose?

This is a test of cause and effect. The analyst is concerned here not so much with whether the results follow in logic and time but in actuality.

C3: Is the stated consequence actually a statement of purpose? See P10.

C4: Are both short-term and long-term consequences considered?

It may be the case that short-term results may affect or inhibit expected long-term results; the potential for such effects must be considered.

Evaluating Consequences for Fair-mindedness

C5: Are positive aftereffects of achieving the purpose comprehensively identified?

Making sure that all positive results have been identified assures that the benefits to be gained by achieving the purpose are fully appreciated.

C6: Are negative aftereffects (results) of achieving the purpose comprehensively identified?

This is to assure that all negative results have been identified so that drawbacks to achieving the purpose are fully anticipated and understood. Identifying drawbacks also provides the analyst with advance warning as to the likely consequences of achieving some purpose. This enables the analyst to alter or abandon the stated purpose, or perhaps alter the means employed so as to minimize drawbacks.

C7: Are the positive consequences of not achieving the purpose comprehensively identified?

By prompting consideration of other purposeful alternatives, the analyst is caused to consider other roads to follow that may not have been clear or obvious until the act of assembling and/or evaluating a completed analysis caused an alternative to surface. This question is an example of how MECA/SM can promote creative thinking.

C8: Are the negative consequences of not achieving the purpose comprehensively identified?

By confronting the negative results of non-achievement of the purpose, the analyst is prompted to consider alternatives. For example, in a workshop with a group of high-school and college career counselors, we engaged in an extended discussion of the likely results of someone's not achieving their stated purpose of entering a given profession and thereby being made unable to earn a living in their chosen field. The counselors identified these conventional and likely results: frustration, depression, alienation, and perhaps the need to rely on public support. Then one of the counselors suggested that the individual might consider starting their own business. This positive consideration, in the context of the originally stated purpose ("to obtain a job in a career area of choice"), probably would not have come to mind had the negative consequences of not achieving the purpose been left unexplored.

Recycling the Results of an Evaluation

If your evaluation results in significant findings, these findings become a part of the analysis. From a teacher's standpoint, this can be done by commenting directly on the analysis or by adding a list of notes to the analysis. From a teacher's or a student's standpoint, if you are evaluating your own analysis, then the analysis should be updated to reflect your valuative findings. In the scientific method, this is called "revising the hypothesis."

Revising an analysis based on one's evaluation accomplishes two things: 1) Revision consolidates the analyst's critical understanding of the material reviewed. 2) Revision provides the reader of an analysis with a more informed basis for critically understanding the material analyzed.

7 How to Use MECA/SM Methodology in Your Classroom

Building the Analytical Classroom

Before you introduce the subject matter of a course of study, introduce your class to the process of critical thinking and the basics of MECA/SM methodology. When I present MECA/SM to a class for the very first time, I start by talking along these lines:

> One of the reasons for attending class is to learn how to think for yourself. Without that ability, while you may gain a limited understanding of a situation, you may also let others who do not have your interests in mind mislead you or take advantage of you. The ability to think for yourself helps you to understand and analyze new situations, evaluate ideas and points-of-view, and solve problems. This kind of thinking is called "critical thinking." The ability to think for yourself helps you make good decisions in your personal, social, and professional lives. You can also think critically about the subject matter you study. Learning to think critically about the subjects you study will help you deal with all kinds of issues in your everyday life. It doesn't matter which course you study; any subject has the potential to develop your thinking skills. All subjects can be analyzed so that you can understand, evaluate, and resolve.

Next, I use a variation of Bloom's taxonomy, called "the thinking ladder." (Maiorana, 1980, p. 240) I draw a six-step ladder on the board and, providing examples step-by-step, engage the class in discussion.

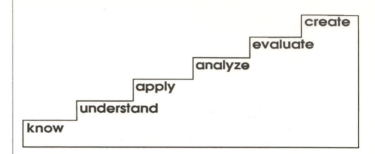

Each step is labeled, starting at the bottom with "know" (in the sense of recalling information) and proceeding up through understand, apply, analyze, evaluate, and create. Indicating that critical thinking usually starts with the second step, I say that there are many ways to think critically, and one such approach is called "means-ends analysis."

Without labeling the discussion as such or burdening my class with the technical jargon of MECA/SM, I then engage the students in a means-ends analysis by asking a series of questions starting with "purpose." I use *their* answers to construct the tennis analysis shown on p. 67. I then supply a title for the analysis, and I label its parts: *Purpose, Resources, Activities*, and *Consequences*. With the tennis analysis on the board, I ask the class to draw on their prior knowledge and understanding to construct a similar model for attending school or college. I encourage students to work together in developing the analyses. Sample models are put on the board and evaluated.

At this point, and along with homework assignments to develop experience-based analyses on topics that they select, the stage has been set to discuss course content in means-ends terms. The students can now, on a basic level, conduct their own means-ends analyses.

Here is a procedure you can follow when presenting new subject matter to students in a means-ends format. The analyses that you present can be based on your expertise in the field, on textbook material, or a combination of the two.

Presenting Subject Matter Analytically

1. *Before class*, prepare MECA/SM analyses of the subject matter to be discussed. If you are to help students develop the cognitive skills that MECA/SM engenders, you must first engage in the strategy to understand how it works. The wedding of MECA/SM methodology in your mind with your own command of the subject matter will lead to good effects and affects for your students.

2. Tell your class that you are going to discuss the topic in a manner that promotes critical thinking.

3. To activate their prior learning, have your students find in their notebooks previous MECA/SM models that you and/or they have developed.

4. Remind them that an analysis is developed by using the Purpose-Resources-Activities-Consequences (PRAC) framework.

5. Sketch a *blank* MECA/SM template on the board.

6. Have your students turn to a new page in their notebooks and copy your blank form from the board.

7. Title the diagram.

8. State the purposes of the subject matter under discussion, and enter that purpose/those purposes under *Purpose* in the analysis.

9.   Continue your discussion through the *Resources* and *Activities* portions of the analysis.

10. Ask your class to evaluate for possible *Consequences*; help them if they have trouble seeing possible results.

11. Ask your students to swap notebooks with their neighbors, and have them evaluate each others' analyses for clarity and completeness. By doing this, you will also be setting the stage for later in the term when they develop their own original analyses. Depending on the material under discussion, evaluations for fair-mindedness may also be made at this time.

12. When you test on the material, base some of your questions on the analyses that you developed in class. It is relatively easy to construct objective and fill-in-the-blank test items based on an analysis. You can also prepare a narrative of about 100 words, include the narrative in the test, and ask the students, through individual test items, to respond in terms of purpose, resources, activities, and consequences.

Developing an Analysis While Making Effective Use of Students' Answers

When developing an analysis on the board, do not hesitate to discuss points that are related to the analysis but are not actually part of the present analysis. This has mainly to do with providing background material or specific examples. For example, if you are analyzing the text of Lincoln's Gettysburg Address (the text of the speech and an analysis appear on pp. 132-134, you might mention that another person was actually the featured speaker of the occasion. He spoke elegantly but tediously for about two hours, whereas Lincoln's talk was quite brief.

If a student anticipates you, and suggests something for the analysis that you plan to mention later, immediately include that suggestion in the analysis (if possible using the actual words of the student), even though it temporarily takes you out of the PRAC procedure. One of the main aims of MECA/SM methodology is to engage students directly in thinking. When suggestions come spontaneously, accept and use them. I even go so far as to take a suggestion which may be way off the mark, help the student refine the suggestion, and then add it to the analysis. Be aware that suggestions will sometimes be made that belong in the analysis but are not now present in your version of the analysis. Include these suggestions, as appropriate, and be sure to update your own notebook. I've done this more than a few times; teachers learn a lot from their students.

I've done this more than a few times; teachers learn a lot from their students.

When asking for entries for the *Consequences* portion of the analysis, I promote a discussion of both positive and negative results. Include comments that you may not agree with but which make sense in the context of the discussion. MECA/SM promotes active intellectual engagement. For this reason, students, free as they often are from conventional wisdom about the topic under discussion, are likely to provide novel, imaginative, and unexpected viewpoints. One student, in connection with a course on public speaking, developed a MECA/SM analysis based on a textbook chapter that addressed outlining a speech. One of her comments for the *Consequences* portion of the analysis was that spending too much time on the outline may limit the time for rehearsing the speech itself.

Focus your delivery on the development of the analysis. When first introduced to MECA/SM, some students fail to reflect the title of the analysis in their notes, and they omit the terms *Purpose, Resources, Activities,* and *Consequences* as headings. Move around the room and make sure that your students' notes accurately reflect the analysis that you and the class are developing on the board.

Having Students Prepare and Present Their Own Analyses

After you have introduced your students to the basics of critical thinking, and have presented several in-class experience-based and content-based MECA/SM analyses, and after they have developed several analyses by themselves by reconstructing their existing store of knowledge, it will be time for your students to develop their own content-based analyses.

Start by using a single paragraph; then build to the point at which they analyze a whole chapter. Have several of the analyses put on the board for class discussion. If you ask for original content-based analyses too early in the term, you will get decidedly mixed results. After your class has become adept at constructing their MECA/SM analyses from experiences, you can ask for original content-based analyses. Some students will take easily to the analysis; others will not. When organizing groups to work on analyses, make sure that those who have demonstrated an understanding early become members of different working groups.

I make it a practice to ask students to write a corresponding narrative for any analysis that they develop. This is one way to develop writing skills regardless of the subject being studied. (See Chapter 8 for more information on writing narratives.)

When writing narratives, students can see for themselves that they already, inherently possess critical faculties:

- They actually have the ability, when they encounter a crystallized description of a situation or topic, to analyze the matter using their own critical-thinking abilities, and come to a refined analytical, critical understanding of the subject.

- They can analytically transform subject matter and then write critically in their own words about that subject matter.

- They can take a given topic and make it their own.

- They can become independent learners with less need to rely extensively on teachers and textbooks for their understanding. This realization on the part of students of their own cognitive abilities goes beyond intellectual empowerment in the classroom; the implications for overall scholastic persistence and achievement, workplace performance, and lifelong learning, are enormous.

Pedagogical Strategies for Employing MECA/SM

Means-ends analysis can be used to analyze a sentence, paragraph, topic, chapter, book, textbook, and on up to a whole body of knowledge. MECA/SM possesses great flexibility, and it opens up a variety of potential classroom applications. In addition to the procedures described above, the following approaches can also be used:

a. Supply a partially completed analysis and have your students review the associated textbook chapter or other material to discover the remaining parts.

b. Mix up the entries on a completed analysis and have your students correctly rearrange the analysis. (This approach is especially effective when used with groups of students.)

c. Supply two or three of the analytical parts, and have your students infer the missing parts without reference to other materials.

d. Provide a completed model, and ask them to write a descriptive narrative.

e. Analyze a newspaper or magazine article to determine whether the piece represents a well-founded discourse or a biased presentation.

f. Promote creative thinking by supplying a blank model with or without a title. Or provide a few scattered entries, subject to wide interpretation, and then have your students complete the analysis. Be prepared to be very accepting of the responses to the creative approach. Evaluate these analyses on their own internal consistency, not on what you yourself might have done beginning at the same starting point.

Regardless of which approach you use (or otherwise develop), it is important to have students share their work with one another as a way to learn more about the means-ends process itself. Sharing also allows students to exercise their ability to evaluate the work of others within a means-ends framework, to recognize that there can be more than one right answer to a given problem, and to collaborate in critical thinking—a style of group problem-solving that is essential in a democratic society.

Reading and Writing with MECA/SM

You can use the following procedure for analyzing textbook chapters. You do not need any prior knowledge of the topics contained in a chapter. You can use this procedure the first time you look at a chapter. The following instructions are worded with teachers in mind, addressing their students:

1. Select a chapter in a textbook.

2. Read only the main headings. Start with the title of the chapter, and read only the *main* topic headings as you turn the pages.

3. Starting with the chapter title, prepare a hand-written list of all the main headings.

4. Identify (mark) each heading in the list as either *Purpose, Resource, Activity,* or *Consequence,* or with a questions mark. (You will resovlve any marked questions in step 6.) The purpose of the subject matter itself may not be identified as such. Look for statements in the early paragraphs that begin with the word "to."

5. Sketch out a blank MECA/SM template, and transfer your markings and findings to it.

6. Read only the first paragraph under each main topic heading, and identify additional elements of *Purpose, Resource, Activity,* or *Consequence.* You may lightly mark the words and phrases in the paragraph itself with the letters P, R, A, or C. If the book does not belong to you, you should eventually erase the pencilings.

7. Transfer your markings and your findings to your MECA/SM diagram.

8. The chapter that you are analyzing may not contain all the necessary MECA/SM elements; however, this does not prevent you from making and completing an analysis to the degree possible. In these instances, you can try to infer any missing elements by yourself or seek the assistance of your teacher. Even if your teacher is not familiar with MECA/SM strategy, you can show your analysis and ask for assistance on any elements that may be missing. If you are going to show someone else one of your analyses, make sure that it is neatly prepared and clearly written or typed.

9. Consider rewriting your diagram to achieve a more logical arrangement. (See the discussion on logical re-arrangement in Chapter 8.)

10. At this point you may engage in pathway analysis. (See the discussion of analytical pathways in Chapter 6.)

Writing a Term Paper with MECA/SM

High school and college students, student teachers, inservice teachers, and graduate students are often required to prepare and write research and term papers. Here is how to use MECA/SM to prepare an outline for these papers:

1. Prepare a blank MECA/SM template. Put *Consequences* near the bottom of the page thereby leaving maximum space to list *Activities*.

2. Enter a title.

3. Enter a statement of purpose that begins with "to."

4. For *Resources*, enter all those references that you will use to help put the paper together: class notes, textbooks, magazine articles, and so on. Some or all of these entries will later form the basis for the report's bibliography.

5. Enter, in topical outline form or simply as a list, all the points you plan to cover. These are *Activities* you are describing, actions that you plan to take for the most important person in a written communication: your reader. Because they are activities, instead of entering "introduction" (a noun, not a verb of action), enter "*provide* introduction." The next entry might be "*describe* the purpose of the (subject)." The next entry might be "*describe* the parts of the (subject)," perhaps with subdivisions like these:

"*tell* about (part a)," "*tell* about (part b)," "*show* a picture (of part c)." Continue in this manner until you have accounted for all activities. In effect, you are making a series of promises to the reader. You are preparing a list of actual actions that you plan to take, not merely a list of static and otherwise abstract topics. Stating outline topics as a series of *Activities* helps you to accomplish the following:

- ◆ identify what those topics should be

- ◆ clarify what you want to convey

- ◆ achieve logical arrangement for your thoughts

- ◆ help the reader seem like a real person with whom you are communicating

[Hint: Assume that you have previously analyzed the digestive system with MECA/SM and prepared an analysis, such as the one shown on page 76. *All* of that analysis, from *Purpose* through *Consequences*, could appear in the *Activities* portion of the analysis you are now developing.]

6. Complete the *Consequences* portion of the diagram. These results are with respect to the purpose stated in step 3: "The purpose of this paper is to discuss (the topic)." Describe what positive things could happen if you achieve your purpose, and what negative things could happen if you do not achieve your purpose, (e.g., pass the course, write a publishable paper, communicate something about the topic). These considerations can be made at least with respect to yourself and/or the reader.

Having prepared the outline, you are now in a position to write the first draft of the paper. Because of the nature of MECA/SM analysis, your paper is likely to be balanced, organized, well-formed, and comprehensive. It will also be critically constructed if the *Activities* portion of your MECA/SM term paper outline is itself based on a MECA/SM analysis of whatever subject you are discussing.

General Use of MECA/SM

You may employ MECA/SM at any time to engage in organized, critical, and creative thought. During a noisy brainstorming session attended by student leaders from various campuses concerning a budget crisis within the university, one student, an active participant in student government at his college, was able to focus the meeting on desired objectives through MECA/SM. This same student, during a "crisis management meeting" with the president of the student government and the dean of students, boasted that he "effectively used MECA/SM analysis to focus and present our ideas to the college administration."

As many students have done, you may also use MECA/SM to reconstruct class notes, newspaper columns and magazine articles; to prepare outlines for term papers, research papers, and class speeches; to organize and manage the activities of your school club or governing organization; and to help focus the energy and thought of your school, club, or community meetings.

8 Critical Thinking across the Curriculum with MECA/SM

MECA/SM analyses have been developed by teachers and students for a wide variety of curriculum areas including *humanities* (education, English, history, language, and music), *natural sciences* (biology, chemistry, geography, geology, mathematics, physics, and physiology), *social sciences* (counseling, economics, geography, health, and psychology), and the *career* and *technology* areas (architecture, business, computers, electrical technology, mechanical technology, and nursing). This chapter is a collection of sample analyses in some of these areas. Both experience-based and text-based MECA/SM analyses are included. Comments accompany each illustration. Summary comments appear in boxes at the top of an analysis; extended comments sometimes follow an analysis. These comments serve two purposes: They interpret the analysis with respect to how well it truly reflects MECA/SM methodology, and they point out the pedagogical implications of using MECA/SM with regard to issues such as planning, prior learning, and motivation.

The analyses should be read, as least initially, in the sequence Topic/Purpose/Resources/Activities/Consequences. Notice, as you ponder each representation, that you gain a better understanding not only of means-ends analysis itself but also of the subject matter represented.

Try to focus on this idea: You are learning the subject matter, and you are learning it within a cognitively critical framework. This feature of simultaneity, this merging of process and product, is what largely accounts for the ability of the MECA/SM analyst to deal with subject matter and critical thinking at the same time. This is the genius of MECA/SM: It teaches the thinker to think critically while communicating subject-matter content simultaneously.

Establishing Purposeful Statements

Conventional learning objectives have a strong hold on the thinking of teachers and students alike (See Chapter 3 for a discussion of the ways that learning objectives inhibit analytical thought). Analysts new to MECA/SM tend to confuse "learning objectives" with "statements of purpose." The following examples help establish the distinction between the two.

COMMENT: *"Learning objectives" have a strong hold on teachers, and they get in the way of teaching for critical thinking. This analysis, a teacher's first try during an inservice workshop on MECA/SM, demonstrates this point; it is not true MECA/SM analysis. Notice that the purpose is stated as a conventional learning objective, does not begin with "to," and is a statement <u>about</u> the subject matter rather than arising from within the subject matter itself; thus, the <u>Purpose</u> statement inhibits a critical train of thought from developing. Can you spot misplaced <u>Resources</u>?*

Analyst: Inservice workshop participant
Subject: Physiology   *Topic:* The human body
Source of raw material: Experience

Title: MECA/SM Analysis of the Functioning of the Human Body (Version 1)

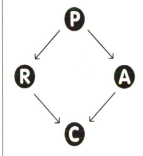

1) PURPOSE (Why?)

The student shall understand the healthy functioning of the human body as well as how and why these processes can go awry, resulting in ill health.

2) RESOURCES (What is needed?)
- inorganic
  - solar/sun
  - earth/minerals
  - water
  - air
- organic
  - carbohydrates
  - proteins
  - lipids
  - acids (RNA and DNA)

3) ACTIVITIES (What is done?)
- chemical reactions <u>plus</u> cycles
- genetic determination <u>plus</u> DNA control
- cells <u>plus</u> receptors
- systems
  - circulation
  - digestion
  - respiration
  - excretion
  - immune system functioning

4) CONSEQUENCES (What can happen if purpose is achieved?)

(None provided by analyst)

COMMENT: The major flaw is that the purpose is about the subject matter and not drawn from within the subject matter itself. In other words, the stated purpose inappropriately substitutes the purpose of the teacher for the purpose of the subject matter. Subject matter exists apart from teachers and students; it exists to serve its own purposes, not those of the people who teach and study it. It is of the utmost importance that this distinction be understood and applied when we perform a means-ends analysis (See Chapter 3).

Otherwise, this analysis is generally accurate in respect to <u>Resources</u> and <u>Activities</u>, though there are a few problems: (a) Cells and cell receptors are resources, but they are shown under <u>Activities</u>. (b) The <u>Activities</u> can be more logically arranged. (c) <u>Purpose</u> includes a statement of "...resulting in ill health," a consequence. After discussing these points, the analyst revised the analysis, producing "Version 2."

Subject matter exists apart from teachers and students; it exists to serve its own purposes, not those of the people who teach and study.

COMMENT: *The problems in Version 1 are corrected in Version 2. The revised analysis has a proper statement of purpose. The cells and cell receptors have been properly identified as* <u>Resources</u>, *not* <u>Activities.</u> *The* <u>Activities</u> *have been organized more logically.* <u>Consequences</u> *are now stated that involve both achieving and not achieving the stated purpose. Whereas Version 1 was burdened with pedagogical convention, Version 2 is in the service of critical analysis of the subject matter itself.*

Analyst: Inservice workshop participant
Subject: Physiology   *Topic:* The human body
Source of raw material: Experience

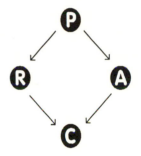

Title: MECA/SM Analysis of the Functioning of the Human Body (Version 2)

(1) PURPOSE (Why?)
to function healthfully in its environment

2) RESOURCES (What is needed?)
- Inorganic
  - solar/sun
  - earth/minerals
  - water
  - air
- Organic
  - carbohydrates
  - proteins
  - lipids
  - acids (RNA and DNA)
  - cells
  - cell receptors

3) ACTIVITIES (What is done?)
- General
  - chemical reactions
  - cell decay
  - cell reproduction
- Specific
  - respiration
  - circulation
  - digestion
  - excretion
  - immunization

(4) CONSEQUENCES (What can happen if purpose is achieved?)
- POSITIVE
  - If purpose is achieved, expectations can be fulfilled.
- NEGATIVE
  - If purpose is not achieved, illness and a reduced capacity to fulfill expectations may result.

Arranging Entries in Logical Order

Usually, the *Resources* and *Activities* portions of a MECA/SM analysis contain the largest number of entries. When developing an analysis, make *Resources* and *Activities* entries in the order that they occur to you (if the analysis is experienced-based), or in the order you come to them (if text-based). The object is to get the ideas down in writing. You can reorder them later for improved logical flow. The next two illustrations make this point. Notice that related activities are not grouped. For example, why not group all the activities associated with air conditioners?

Analyst: Student, Queensborough Community College
Subject: Science   *Topic:* Human Allergies
Source of raw material: Newsletter article: "Allergy Patients Can Work to Control Allergen Quantities." *LungLine,* fall, 1991, page 3.

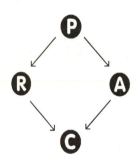

Title: MECA/SM Analysis of the article "Allergy patients can work to control allergen quantities." (Version 1)

1) PURPOSE (Why?)

to reduce the amount of allergens such as house dust, dust mites, and animal dander in their environment

2) RESOURCES (What is needed?)

- humidifers
- air conditioners
- plastic casings
- hot water
- approved chemicals
  - ◆ Acrosan
  - ◆ Allergy Control Solution
- charcoal filters
- High-Efficiency-Particulate-Air (HEPA) filters

3) ACTIVITIES (What is done?)

- humidifiers should not be routinely used
- keep humidity down to 20-30% to keep mites and molds from thriving
- close doors and windows
- keep pets outdoors
- reduce mite population with air conditioners
- reduce levels of pollen and mold in hot weather
- cover mattresses and pillows

- biweekly hot-water laundering of blankets and sheets with chemicals
- acknowledge animal allergy
- remove pets
- limit exposure to animals
- keep pets out of specific rooms
- clean carpets
- denature dust-mite fecal material and animal dander
- remove nitrous oxide and formaldehyde from the air by filtration
- remove moisture from air through air conditioners

4) CONSEQUENCES (What can happen if purpose is achieved?)

- POSITIVE

- patients have fewer allergic reactions
- patients have fewer asthma attacks
- patients take less medication; side effects from medication are lowered
- patients make fewer visits to hospital and doctor
- medical bills are reduced
- patient's environment is cleaner and healthier for self and family
- environment is more comfortable
- complications from allergy and asthma attacks reduced
- patient is healthier
- patient loses fewer work/school days
- patient's mental outlook is better

- NEGATIVE

- high cost of purchasing air conditioners, dehumidifiers, chemicals, plastic covers, etc.
- cleaning and laundering procedures are time- consuming
- sleeping on plastic-covered pillow and mattress might be uncomfortable
- removing favorite pet may be emotionally difficult and stressful
- patients must have knowledge of use of chemicals and machines
- chemicals might be misused
- if humidity is not controlled, mites and molds will increase

COMMENT: *In Version 2, related activities are grouped and arranged in a way that is more logical and easier to understand. What other rearranging was accomplished?*

As you review Version 2, notice the degree of topic consolidation that has taken place. The resources are now grouped under five main entries, giving better form and order to the nine entries in Version 1. In Version 2, there are now eight main activities, giving better form to the 16 entries in Version 1. A similar cogency has been developed for the consequences. Recording of topics within a MECA/SM diagram enhances MECA/SM's usefulness to an analyst in reconstructing material within a critical framework, even when the text on which the analysis was based was conceived hazily and written poorly.

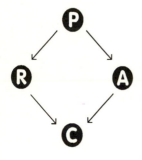

Analyst: Student, Queensborough Community College
Subject: Science   *Topic:* Human Allergies
Source of raw material: Newsletter article: "Allergy Patients Can Work to Control Allergen Quantities." *LungLine,* fall, 1991, page 3.

Title: MECA/SM Analysis of the article "Allergy patients can work to control allergen quantities." (Version 2)

1) PURPOSE (Why?)
to reduce the amount of allergens such as house dust, dust mites, and animal dander in their environment

2) RESOURCES (What is needed?)
- appliances
  - humidifiers
  - air conditioners
- filters
  - charcoal
  - High-Efficiency-Particulate-Air (HEPA) filter
- approved chemicals
  - Acrosan
  - Allergy Control Solution
- hot water

3) ACTIVITIES (What is done?)
- humidifiers should not be routinely used
- keep humidity down to 20-30% to keep mites and molds from thriving
- use air conditioners
  - to remove moisture from air
  - to reduce mite population
  - to reduce levels of pollen and mold in hot weather
  - close doors and windows

- plastic casings
  - protect bedding material
    - cover mattresses and pillows
    - launder blankets and sheets with hot water and chemicals biweekly
  - acknowledge animal allergy
    - remove pets
    - limit exposure to animals
    - keep pets outdoors
    - keep pets out of specific rooms
  - clean carpets, furniture, and bedding with approved chemicals
  - denature dust-mite fecal matter and animal dander
  - remove nitrous oxide and formaldehyde from the air by filtration

4) CONSEQUENCES (What can happen if purpose is achieved?)
- POSITIVE

patients
- have fewer allergic reactions
- have fewer asthma attacks
- take less medication; side effects from medication are lowered
- make fewer visits to hospital and doctor
- environment is cleaner and healthier for self and family
- are healthier
- lose fewer work/school days
- mental outlook is better
  - medical bills are reduced
  - environment is more comfortable
  - complications from allergy and asthma attacks reduced

- NEGATIVE
  - high cost of purchasing air conditioners, dehumidifiers, chemicals, plastic covers, etc.
  - cleaning and laundering procedures are time-consuming

- ◆ sleeping on plastic-covered pillow and mattress might be uncomfortable
- ◆ removing favorite pet may be emotionally difficult and stressful
- ◆ chemicals
  - ■ patients must know how to use chemicals and machines
  - ■ chemicals might be misused
- ◆ if humidity is not controlled, mites and molds will increase

Experience-based Analyses

Analyses in this section are based on analyzing one's existing knowledge. Experiential analysis provides students with a practical basis for immediate practice in MECA/SM methodology, but a larger purpose is also served. Experiential analysis allows one to place knowledge gained through rote learning within a cognitively critical framework. This critical reconstruction has the following positive effects:

1. Students learn that they already possess an ability to think critically.

2. Analysts (teachers and students) learn to focus on the purposes served by subject matter.

3. Analysts examine long-held beliefs, perceptions, and understandings that were gained without benefit of critical reflection.

COMMENT: *This analysis is of special interest because it shows how MECA/SM can incorporate other conventional approaches into a critical-thinking framework. Inspection of the Activities portion of the analysis reveals that it is actually a variation of the classic problem-solving procedure. It is important to make the connection between systematic problem-solving in one learned area and in another. Regardless of the subject matter, the procedure is essentially the same construct as originally envisioned by John Dewey. (See Chapter 3 for further discussion on systematic problem-solving.)*

Analyst: Alexandria Tarasko and Donna Dirico, Teachers,
        Queensborough Community College
Subject: Health   *Topic:* Nursing
Source of raw material: Experience

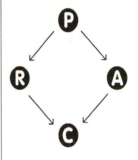

Title: MECA/SM Analysis of Nursing

1) PURPOSE (Why?)
to help patients reach their optimal state of health

2) RESOURCES (What is needed?)
- patient
- patient data
- registered nurse
- health-care facility

3) ACTIVITIES (What is done?)
- collect data (objective and subjective)
- analyze data
- formulate a diagnosis
- decide on realistic goals and outcomes
- plan appropriate interventions
- evaluate effectiveness of interventions

4) CONSEQUENCES (What can happen if purpose is achieved?)
patient: quality of life is improved
nurse: able to meet patient's needs

COMMENT: *Beyond its usefulness as a means to discuss subject matter while simultaneously developing cognitive skills, MECA/SM can be of pedagogical use to teachers in still another way: stirring up students' awareness of their prior knowledge. Too often, topics are addressed in class without the students' awareness of their own prior knowledge. Students may not be ready for new subject matter because their prior learning is insufficient, or because the teacher assumes that more prior learning has taken place than is in fact the case. By requiring that resources be identified, teachers can determine what prior knowledge students possess.*

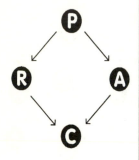

Analyst: Ann Camille Mingione, Teacher, East Islip Junior High School

Subject: English   *Topic*: Paragraph Writing

Source of raw material: Experience

Title: MECA/SM Analysis of Paragraph Writing

1) PURPOSE (Why?)

to express and support a topic in an organized fashion

2) RESOURCES (What is needed?)

- topic
- ability to construct sentences
- ability to gather supporting details

3) ACTIVITIES (What is done?)

- construct an appropriate topic sentence
- construct supporting sentences
- construct an appropriate concluding sentence

4) CONSEQUENCES (What can happen if purpose is achieved?)

- POSITIVE

  - the person who reads the paragraph gains understanding of, and information about, the topic

- NEGATIVE

  - the person who reads the paragraph may be confused, may not gain understanding, and perhaps will be misinformed

COMMENT: *Here is a sentence analysis following upon the preceding paragraph analysis. Teachers and curriculum designers may develop a whole series of MECA/SM analyses, pedagogical pathways, that will help assure that students' work is built on a firm foundation of prior understanding.*

Analyst: Ann Camille Mingione, Teacher, East Islip Junior High School

Subject: English   *Topic:* Sentence Writing
Source of raw material: Experience

Title: MECA/SM Analysis of Sentence Writing

1) PURPOSE (Why?)

to express a complete thought in writing

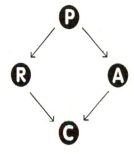

2) RESOURCES (What is needed?)

- thought
- appropriate words
- dictionary

3) ACTIVITIES (What is done?)

- construct a sentence
  - select subject(s)
  - select verb(s)
  - use appropriate punctuation
  - use appropriate capitalization

4) CONSEQUENCES (What can happen if purpose is achieved?)

- POSITIVE
  - a person who reads the sentence can understand the thought.

- NEGATIVE
  - a person who reads the sentence may not understand the thought

COMMENT: *Here is an analysis that provides students with an overview of the subject matter they are to study. After introducing students to critical thinking and the fundamentals of MECA/SM, this analysis could serve as the first one to address actual course content. This style of analysis can be quite useful to students and teachers alike in gaining a critical overall understanding of a subject at the very beginning of the course. Critical, analytical understanding sparks interest and stimulates motivation.*

Analyst: Marietta Cleckley, Science Teacher, Roosevelt Junior/Senior High School

Subject: Science   *Topic:* Chemistry

Source of raw material: Experience

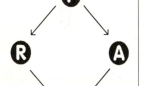

Title: MECA/SM Analysis of Chemistry

1) PURPOSE (Why?)
to research and solve problems related
to the physical nature of things;
to develop new materials and medicines

2) RESOURCES (What is needed?)
- matter
- a problem to solve
- laboratory
- equipment

3) ACTIVITIES (What is done?)
- research the problem
- apply appropriate laws and theories to problem
- make explanations and predictions
- test predictions in laboratory
- draw conclusions

4) CONSEQUENCES (What can happen if purpose is achieved?)
- POSITIVE
quality of life improved

- NEGATIVE
new products can harm people and the environment

Analyst: Victor P. Maiorana, Teacher, Queensborough
    Community College
Subject: Education   *Topic:* Teaching
Source of raw material: Experience

Title: MECA/SM
Analysis of Teaching

1) PURPOSE (Why?)
to help students gain competency, awareness,
and critical understanding of subject matter;

to help students develop basic, critical, and workplace skills

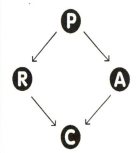

2) RESOURCES (What is needed?)
- students
- subject matter
- teacher's knowledge and understanding of subject matter
- teacher's knowledge and understanding of teaching strategies
- texts and other forms of educational technology
- proper setting

3) ACTIVITIES (What is done?)
- identify material to be taught
- identify teaching and learning strategy
- design lesson plan
- deliver lesson
- assess student achievement
- review material as necessary
- assess lesson plan design
- alter lesson plan as necessary

4) CONSEQUENCES (What can happen if purpose is achieved?)
- POSITIVE
  - student: basic and critical understanding of subject matter studied, development of cognitive skills, development of workplace skills
  - teacher: satisfaction and deeper understanding of subject matter
  - schools and colleges: fulfillment of their mission
  - society: becomes better informed; citizens are better prepared to live in a democracy

• NEGATIVE
- student: poor basic skills, limited understanding of subject matter, poor cognitive and workplace skills
- teacher: frustration, withdrawal, abandonment of teaching
- schools and colleges: inability to fulfill their mission
- society: poorly informed and uncritical citizens; democratic way of life threatened and perhaps lost

Text-based Analyses

Analyses in this section are based on textual material. Text-based analysis provides a practical basis for gaining a timely overview of material, but a much more significant purpose is also served. Text-based analysis allows one to reconstruct the non-critical sequential presentation of subject matter, such as that found in textbooks, into a cognitively critical framework. This critical reconstruction has the following positive effects:

- Students discover that they can think critically the first time they encounter new subject matter.

- Analysts focus on the purposes served by subject matter.

- The analyst becomes equipped with a tool to evaluate how well written material has been prepared. Written material may be considered incomplete to the extent that it lacks the elements of purpose, resources, activities, and consequences. The nature of what may be lacking provides the reader-analyst with a critical basis for evaluating both the completeness and the fair-mindedness of the discussion.

- The analyst develops an organized basis for preparing written versions of the material analyzed. MECA/SM analyses are outline narratives that prompt analysts to write within a critical framework, using their own words. Examples of text-based analytical narratives follow. Narratives may also be written from experience-based analyses.

COMMENT: *Although the analysis on page 125 is true to its stated purpose, it shows how MECA/SM can (mistakenly) be used to deal with subject matter in the crystallized manner of rote learning. This analysis reflects a good understanding of the basics of MECA/SM methodology, but it is so bound by traditional approaches to learning that it does little to cast the subject matter within a framework of critical thinking.*

Can you identify the several reasons that cause the following to be not a true MECA/SM analysis of the subject matter itself?

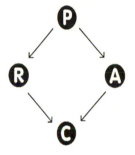

Analyst: Giovanna Riverso, Student, Queensborough
    Community College
Subject: Geology   *Topic:* Earth
Source of raw material: Textbook: C.W. Montgomery,
    Physical Geology, 2nd ed., Wm. C. Brown Pub.,
    1987. Chapter 1, pages 3 to 18.

Title: MECA/SM
Analysis of the Earth (Version 1)

1) PURPOSE (Why?)
To study the earth and the processes that shape it

2) RESOURCES (What is needed?)
- student
- notebook
- textbook
- professor
- wanting to learn

3) ACTIVITIES (What is done?)
- geology as a discipline
- the earth within the universe
- the early earth
- subsequent history
- the modern dynamic earth

4) CONSEQUENCES (What can happen if purpose is achieved?)
- POSITIVE
  - having a basic idea of how the earth came about;
    maybe pursuing a career in earth sciences

- NEGATIVE
  - not being able to understand the basis of earth
    sciences and having to fail the course

COMMENT: *This analysis does not deal dynamically with the subject matter. Notice the following:*

The Purpose *and the* Resources *are the student's own, not the subject matter's.*

Activities *are presented sequentially as they appear in the text, and they are not really activities.*

Consequences *are not that of the subject matter itself.*

This effort is a typical example of what teachers and students do on initial tries at MECA/SM analysis. It is an indication of how deeply ingrained content-theory transmission learning (lecturing and memorizing) is in the educational establishment.

Analyst: Giovanna Riverso, Student, Queensborough
    Community College
Subject: Geology   *Topic*: Earth
Source of raw material: Textbook: C.W. Montgomery,
    Physical Geology, 2nd ed., Wm. C. Brown Pub.,
    1987. Chapter 1, pages 3 to 18.

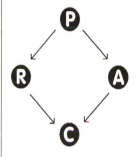

Title: MECA/SM
Analysis of the Earth (Version 2)

1) PURPOSE (Why?)

From the viewpoint of those who inhabit the earth
to meet people's everyday needs and services.

2) RESOURCES (What is needed?)
- land
- air
- atmosphere
- water
- oceans
- the earth's solar system
- planets

3) ACTIVITIES (What is done?)
- maintaining dynamic
  equilibrium
- heating and differentiation
- geological processes
- the effect of the passage of time
- birth and death of stars
- human existence

4) CONSEQUENCES (What can happen if purpose is achieved?)

- POSITIVE
  - if we take care of the earth, then it will pay us back by giving us more resources so we humans can live longer.

- NEGATIVE
  - if we don't take care of the earth, it will die, and so will we.

COMMENT: Determining the purpose of the earth can be construed as a teleological issue, and as such it may have no scientifically probable resolution. In cases like this one, the analyst's challenge is to interpret subject matter in light of the reality of human existence. This student established a purpose for the earth that served some obvious intent, one with which both the teleologically and non-teleologically oriented would agree. Self-centered though they may be, purposes that are rooted in the day-to-day reality of human life provide reasons for learning a topic—reasons that are real, current, and understandable to the student, reasons that MECA/SM helps teachers to identify and present in class.

In Version 2, the student has gained a critical understanding of the earth itself. This is not some arms-length, crystallized understanding promoted by the content-theory-based analysis that underlies Version 1. The Version-2 analysis caused the student to appreciate why she was studying the topic, what importance it held for her herself and for those around her; accordingly, a more thoughtful and enlightened concept of the earth and its dynamic elements is revealed in this version.

A major payoff of MECA/SM analysis can be seen in the student's change of her interpretation of the consequences. Comparing Versions 1 and 2 reveals the very real power of MECA/SM to help the analyst transcend normal content-theory presentations. MECA/SM provides analysts with the ability to adopt an inquiry-based attitude and thereby discover the essential issues that are part of all subject matter.

Because of the importance of Purpose, MECA/SM tends to initiate and foster discussions along teleological lines. Even if one were to excise the teleologically-based purpose shown, the rest of the analysis—from a physical and practical viewpoint—would still be valid.

> **COMMENT:** *This is a good first try. The statements of* <u>Purpose</u> *need work. The* <u>Activities</u> *should be restated using "find" instead of "finding," "gain" instead of "gaining," and so on. The* <u>Consequences</u> *also contain a purpose. An example of a MECA/SM narrative is provided below.*

Analyst: Sharon Beharry, Student, Queensborough Com-
     munity College
Subject: Health   *Topic*: Breaking the Tobacco Habit
Source of raw material: Textbook: D. Hales, *An Invi-*
*   tation to Health*. Benjamin Cummings Pub. Co.,
    1989. Chapter 12.

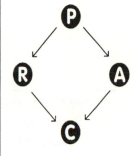

Title: MECA/SM
Analysis of Breaking the Tobacco Habit

1) PURPOSE (Why?)
to help smokers quit smoking
to show how non-smokers are affected, too

2) RESOURCES (What is needed?)
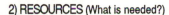
- smoker
- non-smoking friend
- nicotine gum
- diary

3) ACTIVITIES (What is done?)
- finding out if you're hooked
- gaining awareness of diseases associated with smoking
- finding out why you smoke
- helping a smoker to quit
- keeping records
- quitting/cutting down
- seeking therapy

4) CONSEQUENCES (What can happen if purpose is achieved?)

- decrease in the risk of smoke-related diseases
- better health
- cleaner air to breathe

Narrative

The purpose of this chapter is to help smokers quit smoking, and to show non-smokers how they are affected, too, by passive smoke. Resources needed for the(se) purpose(s) are these: a smoker, a non-smoking friend, nicotine gum, and a diary. The activities involved are these: finding out if you're hooked, gaining awareness of diseases associated with smoking, finding out why you smoke, helping a smoker to quit, keeping records, quitting smoking, and seeking therapy. When these two purposes are achieved, there is a decrease in the risk of smoke-related diseases, better health for everyone in society, and cleaner air to breathe.

COMMENT: Notice that the first statement of purpose is simply a restatement of the title; therefore, it does not move the analysis forward. The second statement of purpose is not addressed in the analysis; it should be treated in a separate analysis. The <u>Purpose</u> of this subject representation is actually found in the first part of the <u>Results</u>, and should be stated as "to decrease the risk of smoke-related diseases." The complete thought then becomes "The purpose of breaking the tobacco habit is to decrease the risk of smoke-related diseases." The rest of the <u>Results</u> stated—"better health and cleaner air"—can remain as a consequential statement.

Narratives serve the teacher's purpose of assessing how well students understand both MECA/SM strategy and the subject matter. For example, the first sentence in the foregoing analysis narrative should have begun "The purpose of breaking the tobacco habit is to ...."

Instead, it begins with the non-analytical statement: "The purpose of this chapter is...." This is evidence that the writer, despite statements of purpose to the contrary, slipped into a content-theory mindset when writing the narrative. The purpose changed from that of the subject matter itself to that of the textbook author.

MECA/SM narratives allow any teacher to include writing assignments seamlessly into the instruction of any subject and analysis. Students seem to find writing a narrative a logical next learning step; with the analysis to guide them, they find it a straightforward assignment. In this manner, students improve their skill in preparing written material that is cognitively and consciously critical.

Teachers should not insist that narratives be written in this sequence: purpose/resources/activities/consequences. Give students the freedom to write as they see fit. As long as they are accounted for, the basic elements may be presented in any sequence. Variety adds interest and allows the writer to emphasize different points. Moreover, students write better and more gladly when they are encouraged to express their individuality and speak with their own "voices" in their writing, making their own choices of wording and phrasing. The act of writing a narrative often leads students to think of things that are not in the original analysis. Encourage these developments. A MECA/SM analysis can always be developed a few degrees further.

A MECA/SM analysis can always be developed a few degrees further.

COMMENT: Using MECA/SM to teach history provides a means of actively engaging students in material they too often perceive as boring. The analytical and evaluative aspects of MECA/SM provide the basis for allowing the analyst to determine whether the version of history being read is likely to be complete and fair-minded. Similar analyses have been made for the American *Declaration of Independence* and the speech of Martin Luther King, Jr. "I Have a Dream."

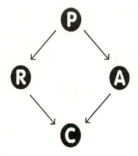

Analyst: Victor P. Maiorana, Teacher, Queensborough Community College

Subject: History   *Topic:* Lincoln's Gettysburg Address

Source of raw material: Harvard Classics, v. 43 p.415

Title: MECA/SM Analysis of Lincoln's Gettysburg Address

1) PURPOSE (Why?)

to achieve a new birth of freedom

2) RESOURCES (What is needed?)
- forefathers
- new nation
- brave men
- people
- beliefs
  (all men are created equal)

3) ACTIVITIES (What is done?)
- engaged in civil war
- testing nation's endurance
- meeting to dedicate a burial ground
- field already dedicated by fallen men
- instead, must have increased devotion to cause
- must resolve that these men did not die in vain

4) CONSEQUENCES (What can happen if purpose is achieved?)
- government of, by, and for the people shall not perish from the earth

> **COMMENT:** *The actual text of the Gettysburg Address follows. Use it to determine whether, using MECA/SM, you would arrive at a similar analysis.*

Fourscore and seven years ago our fathers brought forth on this continent a new nation, conceived in liberty, and dedicated to the proposition that all men are created equal. Now we are engaged in a great civil war, testing whether that nation, or any nation so conceived and so dedicated, can long endure. We are met on a great battlefield of that war. We have come to dedicate a portion of that field as a final resting-place for those who here gave their lives that that nation might live. It is altogether fitting and proper that we should do this. But, in a larger sense, we cannot dedicate—we cannot consecrate—we cannot hallow—this ground. The brave men, living and dead, who struggled here have consecrated it, far above our poor power to add or detract. The world will little note, nor long remember, what we say here, but it can never forget what they did here. It is for us the living, rather, to be dedicated here to the unfinished work which they who fought here have thus far so nobly advanced. It is rather for us to be here dedicated to the great task remaining before us—that from these honored dead we take increased devotion to that cause for which they gave the last full measure of devotion—that we here highly resolve that these dead shall not have died in vain—that this nation, under God, shall have a new birth of freedom—and that government of the people, by the people, for the people, shall not perish from the earth.

COMMENT: *Here is Lincoln's Gettysburg Address in Spanish. Similar versions have been prepared in Chinese, Greek, Italian, and Russian. Perhaps if a concern to develop cognitive skills motivated all educators to teach all students to engage all subject matter analytically, there would be less controversy surrounding initiatives such as English as a Second Language and multiculturalism. The study of language and culture, instead of pointing up differences, could start to emphasize what all people have in common: the potential to think and act in a thorough and fair-minded manner.*

Lincoln's Gettysburg Address in Spanish

Hace ochenta y siete años, nuestros padres fundaron en este continente una nación nueva, concebida en la libertad, y dedicada al principio de que todas las personas son creadas iguales. Ahora estamos envueltos en una gran guerra civil, tratando de averiguar si esta nación, o cualquier otra nación así concebida y dedicada, puede durar mucho tiempo. Nos encontramos en un gran campo de batalla de aquella guerra. Estamos aquí para dedicar parte de aquel campo de batalla como lugar de descanso eterno para aquellos que dieron sus vidas para que la nación pudiera vivir. Es apropiado y justo que hagamos esto. Pero, en un sentido más amplio, no podemos dedicar—no podemos consagrar—no podemos santificar—esta tierra. Los hombres valientes, vivos y muertos, que lucharon aquí la han consagrada, más allá de nuestro pobre poder de aumentar o disminuir su valor. El mundo casi no notará ni recordará lo que estamos diciendo, pero no puede olvidar lo que ellos hicieron aquí. Los que sobrevivimos, por otro lado, tenemos que dedicarnos al trabajo por terminar que los que lucharon han llavado hasta aquí tan noblemente. Nos toca dedicarnos a la gran tarea que aún nos queda—que de estos condecorados muertos aumentemos nuestra devoción a aquella causa por la cual dieron la última prueba de su devoción—que aquí juremos que estos héroes no hayan muerto en vano—que esta nación, bajo Dios, tenga un renacimiento de la libertad, y que el gobierno del pueblo, por el pueblo, para el pueblo, no desaparezca de la tierra.

> **COMMENT:** *Because MECA/SM relies on the structure of human language, one can use it to teach language and critical thinking simultaneously. When applied to a recognized work of literature, two more learning activities are added: reading skills and literature appreciation.*

Analyst: Daniel Garcia, Teacher, West Islip High School

Subject: Literature/Language   *Topic:* Don Quixote/ Spanish

Source of raw material: Miguel de Cervantes: *Don Quixote p. 313*

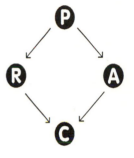

Title: MECA/SM Análisis de una conversacion entre la duquesa y Sancho

1) PROPÓSITO (¿Por qué?)

Intentar hacer que Don Quixote quede en ridículo

2) RECURSOS (¿Qué se necesita?)

- un burro
- Sancho
- la duquesa

- el duque
- Don Quixote

3) ACTIVIDADES (¿Qué se hace?)

- La duquesa le pidió a Sancho que llevara su burro al gobierno.

- Sancho contestó, con gusto, que ya había bastantes burros en el gobierno.

- La duquesa consultó con el duque sobre la manera en que ellos pudieran gastarle unas bromas a Don Quixote.

- La duquesa y el duque concibieron muchas bromas.

4) CONSECUENCIAS (¿Cuál será el resultado si el propósito se logra?)

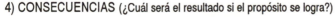

- A Don Quixote le hicieron quedar en ridículo, y las bromas concibidas por la duquesa y el duque eran entre las aventuras primordiales de Don Quixote.

Translation:

Purpose: To try to make Don Quixote look foolish.

Resources: A donkey and Sancho, the Duchess, the Duke, and Don Quixote.

Activities: The Duchess asked Sancho to take her donkey to the government. Sancho replied, with relish, that there were already enough asses in government. The Duchess conferred with the Duke on how to play some joke on Don Quixote. The Duchess and the Duke devised many jokes.

Consequences: Don Quixote was made to look foolish, and the jokes devised by the Duchess and the Duke were among Don Quixote's prime adventures.

Analyst: Teacher, Queensborough Community College
Subject: Addition   *Topic:* Adding 7 apples to 8 apples
Source of raw material: Experience

Title: MECA/SM Analysis of
Adding 7 Apples to 8 Apples

1) PURPOSE (Why?)
to add 7 apples to 8 apples

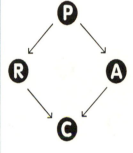

2) RESOURCES (What is needed?)
- knowledge of base-10 system
- a quantity of, or the idea of a quantity of, 7 apples
- a quantity of, or the idea of a quantity of, 8 apples
- paper
- pencil

3) ACTIVITIES (What is done?)
- clearly write the numbers down, one under the other, observing place values and decimals, if any:

$$\begin{array}{r} 7 \\ 8 \\ \hline \end{array}$$

- starting with the right-most column, add the values in that column:

$$\begin{array}{r} 7 \\ 8 \\ \hline 5 \end{array}$$

- if the value exceeds 10 carry the amount of excess, in units of 10, to the next column:

$$\begin{array}{r} 7 \\ 8 \\ 1 \\ \hline 5 \end{array}$$

- repeat procedure for remaining columns:

$$\begin{array}{r} 7 \\ 8 \\ \hline 15 \end{array}$$

4) CONSEQUENCES (What can happen if purpose is achieved?)
- The total number of apples is now represented in summary form.

COMMENT: The <u>Purpose</u>, most of <u>Resources</u>, and the <u>Consequences</u> in this analysis are not discussed in the raw material. These elements were conceived by the MECA/SM analyst. The general lack of purpose, resources, and consequences in math and science classrooms and textbooks is probably a major cause at all levels of students' fear and trouble with mathematics. It turns them away from the study of math and science.

Analyst: Rita Helvelka, Teacher, PS32, Grade 5
Subject: Mathematics   *Topic:* Decimals
Source of raw material: B. Silver, *Mathematics—
    Exploring Your World,* chapter 8.

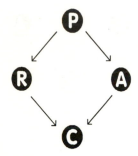

Title: MECA/SM Analysis of Decimals

1) PURPOSE (Why?)

to allow values of less than one to be represented mathematically

2) RESOURCES (What is needed?)

- understanding of the base-10 system
- understanding of basic arithmetic operations
- integers and decimals
- a problem to solve

3) ACTIVITIES (What is done?)

- do the arithmetic
- compare and order the decimals
- evaluate the answer

4) CONSEQUENCES (What can happen if purpose is achieved?)

- values of less than one are accounted for, thus allowing precise representations of numeric values such as those used in physical measurements and accounting for money

COMMENT: *A major point made in the preceding analysis is the importance of the study of understanding of decimals. The subject-matter processes (Activities) are placed in an intellectually motivational context that promotes inquiry and discovery. This analysis would be used to introduce the subject of decimals. The analysis also provides the basis for an analytical pathway that would lead the analyst to the activities of doing the arithmetic, comparing and ordering decimals, and evaluating answers. These nested analyses would each have their own purpose-resources-activities-consequences treatments.*

With respect to learning readiness, this analysis shows the specific intellectual resources that students should already possess before a discussion of decimals is taken up in class. The lack of readiness, which grows more and more critical as students climb the academic ladder, probably accounts for the increasingly poor performance of American students in math and science.

COMMENT: *Mathematics education in schools today tends to be conducted on the basis of "authentic" problems, i.e. real-life, real-world mathematical problems to be solved. Here is an analysis that places the subject matter of mathematics within the framework of an authentic example. The* <u>Consequences</u> *portion allows students to reflect on why solving for a single variable is important. Similar analyses have been made for arithmetic, counting, and the base-10 system.*

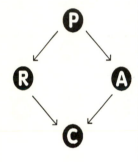

Analyst: Math Teacher, Queensborough Community College

Subject: Mathematics   *Topic*: Solving for a Single Variable

Source of raw material: Experience

Title: MECA/SM
Analysis of Solving for a Single Variable

1) PURPOSE (Why?)
to determine Joan's earnings

2) RESOURCES (What is needed?)
- Tom and Joan's total earnings ($81.00)
- knowledge that Joan earns twice as much as Tom

3) ACTIVITIES (What is done?)
- represent Tom's earnings as X
- represent Joan's earnings as 2X
- relate individual earnings to total earnings:
  $$X + 2X = 81$$
- solve for X:
  $$3X = 81$$
  $$X = 27$$
- solve for Joan's earnings:
  $$X = 27$$
  $$2X = 54$$

4) CONSEQUENCES (What can happen if purpose is achieved?)
- knowledge of Joan's earnings can be used in some practical manner, such as preparing a payroll check for the amount earned, determining Joan's year-to-date earnings, or comparing Joan's earnings with that earned by other people.

> **COMMENT:** *Formulas are often presented in class as givens. Discussions proceed in terms of the formula itself. Students learn how to manipulate a formula with no appreciation of what purpose it serves in the real world. In the case of the formula for a straight line, the formula is presented as a means for drawing a straight line; learning is usually focused on being able to manipulate the formula in an abstract setting. MECA/SM causes the teacher and student to reflect upon why one should care about studying the formula and what consequences follow. By identifying the necessary resources and activities, MECA/SM also helps students gain an appreciation of the intellectual orderliness that must accompany mathematical operations. Math moves from being a mysterious set of abstract and memorized formulations to being a series of logical steps that serve real purposes for real people.*

Analyst: Clara Wajngurt, Mathematics Teacher, Queensborough Community College
Subject: Mathematics   *Topic:* The Straight Line
Basis of Analysis: Experience

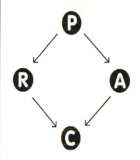

Title: MECA/SM Analysis of the Formula for a Straight Line: Y=MX+B

1) PURPOSE (Why?)
To allow engineers, architects, and scientists to create precise designs

2) RESOURCES (What is needed?)
- M (the coefficient of X)
- B (the Y-intercept)
- values for X

- knowledge of algebra
- ability to make substitutions in an equation
- graph paper, pencil

3) ACTIVITIES (What is done?)
- substitute each X value into the equation to obtain the corresponding X value

- write each answer as an ordered pair
- plot the X and Y points on graph paper
- connect the points to reveal the straight line

4) CONSEQUENCES (What can happen if purpose is achieved)
- Engineers can design machines and bridges; architects can design buildings; scientists can pursue the discovery and development of new knowledge.

COMMENT: *The information for this analysis is spread throughout the raw material, which contains just one topic heading to guide the analyst's identification of major points. Despite this, the student developed an analysis that clearly reveals the strategic considerations that were at play.*

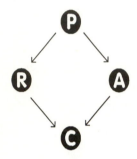

Analyst: Johanna Archi, student, Queensborough Community College

Subject: History   *Topic:* World War II

Source of raw material: Textbook: Keegan, J. *The Second World War.* 1990, pp. 127-33.

Title: MECA/SM Analysis of Germany's Strategy during World War II

1) PURPOSE (Why?)

To help Germany decide which enemy to attack next: Britain or Russia?

2) RESOURCES (What is needed?)	3) ACTIVITIES (What is done?)
• Reports from Abwehr (German Intelligence)	• OKW monitored Soviet capabilities
• OKW Office (war office)	• OKW said Red Army capable but disorganized.
• "Fritz" (Colonel Lossberg's plan to invade Russia)	• Operation Sealion called off on 9/7/40.
• "Sealion" (the plan to invade England)	• Attaché in Moscow reported a 3-to-1 tank advantage in favor of Russia.
• Attaché reports from Moscow	
• Study by Dr. F. Todt, Chief, German War Construction	
• German Economic Planning Authority (EPA)	• Hitler decided he could beat the odds.
• EPA study on economic aspects of war with Russia	• German headquarters for invasion established in East Prussia in August, 1940.
	• Thirty-five German divisions sent to E. Prussia
	• EPA decided that Germany had resources to attack Russia.
	• Some German generals warned of dire consequences.

4) CONSEQUENCES (What can happen if purpose is achieved?)

- POSITIVE

◆ Attacking Russia before it was militarily prepared would bring great benefits to Germany. Recent land acquisitions by Russia, that had enlarged Russia's strategic opportunities while narrowing Germany's, would be stopped.

- NEGATIVE

◆ Some German generals (Manstein and Guderain) feared the "1812 factors" of great space swallowing numbers of soldiers. They felt that a Napoleon-like retreat from Moscow was a real possibility.

COMMENT: *Here is a straightforward analysis that efficiently summarizes the main ideas in the raw material. The analysis reflects management's point-of-view, hence providing the basis for teachers and students to consider how employees and/or unions might view the activities and consequences.*

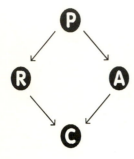

Analyst: Stephen Lane, student, Queensborough Community College

Subject: Business   *Topic*: Human Relations

Source of raw material: Textbook: Rachman

Title: MECA/SM Analysis of Human Relations

1) PURPOSE (Why?)
to improve employee productivity

2) RESOURCES (What is needed?)
- leaders
- communicators
- motivational theories and techniques (Maslow's hierarchy of needs, Hertzberg's hygiene/ motivational factors, results of Hawthorne studies, Theory X and Y)

3) ACTIVITIES (What is done?)
- arrange informal groups
- improve communication
- motivate employees
- set goals
- modify behavior
- retrain
- enrich/redesign jobs
- provide flextime schedule
- share works and jobs

4) CONSEQUENCES (What can happen if purpose is achieved?)
- POSITIVE
  - Increased employee participation and production
  - Increased profits for company
- NEGATIVE
  - Poorly motivated employees and low production levels
  - Decreased profits for company

> **COMMENT:** *The ability of MECA/SM to serve as an integrating medium is shown in this analysis. The student was able to include her own thoughts in the* <u>Consequences</u>; *she brought to the analysis her prior understanding of speech-making when she came to consider negative* <u>Consequences.</u>

Analyst: Student, Queensborough Community College
Subject: Communications　　*Topic:* Giving a Speech
Source of raw material: Textbook: Hamilton, G. *Public Speaking for College and Career.* Chapter 6, "Finding Materials."

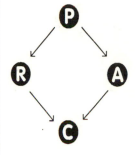

Title: MECA/SM Analysis of Finding Materials

1) PURPOSE (Why?)
To lend credibility and timeliness to one's speech

2) RESOURCES (What is needed?)
- personal experiences and investigations
- library resources
- computer databases
- interviews
- other resources

3) ACTIVITIES (What is done?)
- prepare for interview
- conduct interview
- take notes
- give credit
- evaluate all sources
- find right materials

4) CONSEQUENCES (What can happen if purpose is achieved?)

● POSITIVE
- ◆ * Will help you prepare your speech with correct and important information
- ◆ *You are able to persuade your listening audience to your position

● NEGATIVE
- ◆ *You might collect too much information and go too far into detail, which will bore the members of the audience.

(*=my own ideas)

COMMENT: *In this analysis, the student was able to incorporate material from class notes with information from a textbook to obtain a comprehensive, analytical view of the subject matter. See student's note.*

Analyst: Student, Queensborough Community College
Subject: Marketing   *Topic:* Newspaper Advertising
Source of raw material: Textbook: Russell, J.T. and Lane, R. *Advertising.* Prentice-Hall, 1990, Chapter 8.

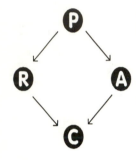

Title: MECA/SM Analysis of Newspapers in Advertising

1) PURPOSE (Why?)
To inform the public of various sales available in the area

2) RESOURCES (What is needed?)
- subscribers
- discounts
- zoned editions
- syndicated supplements
- regional supplements
- local supplements
- supplement network

3) ACTIVITIES (What is done?)
- do market research in field
- determine pricing for advertising
- produce newspaper
- distribute newspaper
- aim at attracting teenagers and young adults

4) CONSEQUENCES (What can happen if purpose is achieved)
- POSITIVE
  - ◆ Less expensive than to advertise in magazines. Shorter lead time–can call today and have ad placed in tomorrow's paper. Can use as test before ad runs nationally.

- NEGATIVE
  - ◆ Short shelf life. Paper thrown away after reader reads what he wants. Read in a hurry. Very competitive with other papers.

NOTE: The above analysis contains information given in class and text.

There you have it: A trip through the curriculum on the cognitive strategy of MECA/SM. Now that you have seen how it works, will you accept the invitation extended in the next chapter?

9 An Invitation

Good teaching methodologies are rare. A methodology that cuts across the curriculum in a manner that directly addresses each unique subject-matter area is unheard of. As an educator, you are probably inherently skeptical of any claim for a single teaching methodology capable of meeting the ideal criteria described in Chapter 4, as, indeed, you should be. As a critical thinker, you should also challenge the criteria themselves, for a critical thinker is one who challenges assumptions, asks questions, puts ideas to the test. A critical thinker is also someone open to innovative and imaginative alternatives.

I invite you to use MECA/SM to think critically about your own subject-matter area or field of expertise. Draw only on your current knowledge and understanding of your field; no books or other reference materials will be needed. By completing the analysis, you will have, perhaps for the first time, a global and *critical* view of your field. Use this analysis as a basis for establishing analytical pathways towards critically informing all your classroom discussions on the subject or subjects that you teach. Most importantly, share these analytical diagrams with your students so that you may truly build an analytical classroom.

An Experience-based MECA/SM Analysis of Your Field of Expertise

Follow the procedure described below, and record your responses in the MECA/SM diagram that follows these instructions:

1. Enter your name as analyst.

2. At "Subject," enter the general name of the subject matter associated with your field or special interest.

3. At "Topic," enter an issue directly associated with the general subject matter. If you want to analyze your whole field (that is, the entry you made in step 2), then skip this step.

4. At "Source of raw material," enter "Experience and Education."

5. Complete the title by adding the name of the subject matter you selected in either step 2 or step 3.

6. Think about the purpose of the subject matter that appears in the *title* of your analysis. What purpose or purposes does it serve? Said differently, what *meaning* does the subject have? Why should anyone care about it? Everything you enter in this analysis is to be drawn from *within* your subject matter itself; it is not to be *about* it. For example, do not ask: "Why do we study biology?" This leads to objective-based responses along the lines of "We study biology to learn about living things, about plants and animals." Ask, instead, what the purpose is of biology itself. Heart muscle beats, eyes see, brain tissue thinks; what purpose does your field/special interest *achieve* when it accomplishes its inherent purpose? Enter your response in the *Purpose* portion of the analysis.

7. Under *Resources*, list all the *static means* (tools, ingredients, elements, or components) that are necessary to achieve the stated purpose.

8. Under *Activities*, identify all the *dynamic means* (processes) by which the resources are employed, or that are otherwise required, to achieve the stated purpose. List them spontaneously as they occur to you. If necessary, you can rearrange them later in logical order.

9. Identify the *Consequences* (effects, results) that are likely to occur when the purpose is actually achieved. At a minimum, identify at least one positive result of achieving the purpose, and ponder as well possible negative results if the purpose is achieved. Consider also the possible positive and negative consequences that might be the outcomes if the purpose is not achieved.

Review your "Version 1" for internal consistency and fair-mindedness (see Chapter 5). Show your MECA/SM analysis to, and discuss it with, a colleague. Do not hesitate to change the analysis, as appropriate. If you want to develop this analysis further, take any entry in the analysis and develop subsequent and related MECA/SM analyses. (see Analytical Pathways in Chapter 6.)

Analyst:
Subject: *Topic:*
Source of raw material:

Title: MECA/SM Analysis of

_____

1) PURPOSE (Why?)

2) RESOURCES (What is needed?)   **3) ACTIVITIES** (What is done?)

-
-
-
-

4) CONSEQUENCES (What can happen if purpose is achieved?)

- POSITIVE
  -
  -

- NEGATIVE
  -
  -

Preparing a narrative allows the analyst to write within a critical framework, provides an opportunity to review the analysis for purposes of modifying or correcting the analysis, and encourages the development of writing skills. (See chapter 8.) The best way to appreciate these benefits is to experience them. Base your narrative on the analysis you have prepared.

A Narrative of Your Analysis

Narrative

_____

_____

_____

_____

_____

_____

_____

_____

_____

_____

_____

_____

_____

_____

_____

_____

_____

10 Principles of Critical Thinking across the Curriculum: Manifesto for the Analytical Classroom

New principles of teaching and learning are needed for the following reasons:

1. Although the public school, the university, and the workplace expect and prize the development and use of critical thinking, reading, writing, speaking, and listening skills, students at all levels do not generally develop these skills.

2. The development of cognitive skills is thwarted by reliance on content-transmission theory, a theory that promotes crystallized teaching and learning of subject matter by relying on the lecture-for-recall method, a method that induces rote learning.

3. Underprepared students are underprepared because they do not possess rote-learning skills. The lecture-for-recall method, because it does not draw on inborn and latent cognitive abilities, places the underprepared at a great learning disadvantage, and it drives them from the classroom.

4. The cognitive development of the prepared student is discouraged by use of the lecture-for-recall method and reliance on rote-learning skills.

5. Teacher education and faculty-development programs continue to operate on philosophical and practical bases that encourage, promote, and as-

sure the continued use of the lecture-for-recall method.

In sum, the problem with American education is not primarily a financial, curricular, assessment, or managerial problem; *it is, rather, a problem of teaching and learning methodology.*

For 2,500 years, content-transmission theory has formed the philosophical and operational basis for European and American educational practice. In earlier days, outside-the-classroom activities in the family, church, and society complemented, and did not compete with, the education and cognitive development of students. The rote-learning effects of content theory were offset through storytelling, book reading, and radio, all of which were cognitively stimulating. Our contemporary electronic media, and other media driven for the most part by the advertising that accompanies them, encourage mindless acceptance, not thoughtful consideration; short-term thinking, not consideration of consequences; quick satisfaction, not a thought-out understanding. In our sensate culture of 10-second sound bytes, photo ops, and pre-packaged conclusions, content theory reasserts its crystalline authority, while the development of basic, cognitive, and workplace skills suffers. In short, educators do not know how to compete for the attention of students, whereas the purveyors of modern electronic media and the modern culture gurus do, and they are winning the battle for our students' attention, time, priorities, and values.

Summary: The Analytical-critical Principles of Teaching and Learning

All teachers, curriculum designers, educational technologists, and administrators must meet their collective responsibility to help educate a citizenry with the ability to understand, analyze, evaluate, and problem-solve in the service of themselves, their families, and the society, in order to protect and preserve our democratic way of life. Only through the development of citizens who can think and act thoughtfully will this responsibility be met.

It is time for a new set of educational principles, principles that will break the hold of content theory. These new principles, collectively an analytical teaching and learning strategy, would stanch the brain drain of modern culture, focus on the development of cognitive skills, and give consumers, viewers, and voters an analytical-critical ability to shovel their way through the rubbish. The term "analytical" is used to represent those cognitive skills that a thoughtful person needs to exercise in order to *be* thoughtful.

Purpose

Intentions and ends-in-view are discovered in the classroom by looking for them in the subject matter itself, the main element that intellectually and socially connects teacher and student.

Reconstruction

All subject matter is raw unless and until it is actively processed in a way that promotes inquiry, discovery, and reconstruction of subject matter.

Simultaneity

The development of basic, critical, and workplace skills must be integrated with the delivery of regular course content.

Methodology

Method is primary to teaching and learning, and it needs to be supported by organization. Teaching-and-learning methodology must be made manifest; that is, it needs to be recognized and understood by students.

Transformation

Students and teachers use the same thinking methods, enabling them to analyze subject matter collaboratively in a manner that encourages intellectual and social transformation.

Up to this point, and primarily because an across-the-curriculum methodology has not been available, it has been operationally impractical to require that *all* teachers engage in the development and deployment of critical-thinking skills. We now have a basis for change. Analytical teaching and learning principles provide the basis for establishing critical thinking across the curriculum in any analytical school or university classroom. These principles, together with a specific analytical methodology like MECA/SM, can guide and inform American classrooms. Starting now and into the 21st century, from grade school through graduate school, the analytical classroom can give American learners what they need to become critical thinkers.

How to Tell If Your Classroom Is an analytical Classroom

Use the following checklist by yourself or with colleagues and students to determine whether classrooms in your school are functioning analytically. The checklist serves two purposes:

1. If you are new to teaching the skills of critical thinking, then use the checklist as a survey of the basics for building an analytical classroom.

2. If you believe that you already teach cognitive skills, then use the checklist to determine how close your classroom comes to being an analytical classroom.

The checklist is based on two main themes. First, the teacher must *consciously* make the effort to discuss subject matter with students within a critical framework. The equally important other main concern is that students are made aware that the subject matter is being presented within a critical framework and that they themselves learn to apply the framework by and for themselves.

Is yours an analytical classroom?

Checklist

ITEM	YES	NO
1. Do you first present subject matter in lecture format before you attempt to engage students in critical thinking about it?		
2. Do you think that your subject matter can be constructed critically?		
3. Do you actually prepare your lesson plan or class notes within the critical strategy that you employ?		
4. Do you actually use critical notes as a basis for delivering subject matter in the class?		
5. If you actually present subject matter in class according to a critical strategy, do you consciously and purposively share that strategy with your students?		
6. Do you teach your students to use the same strategy that you use to construct the subject matter critically?		
7. Can your students apply the strategy to any material chosen at random, and come away with a critical understanding of that material?		
8. Have you evaluated your students' independent analytical efforts and offered constructive comments?		
9. Do you assign independent projects asking students to demonstrate understanding and application of the strategy?		
10. Do your exams contain questions based on critical strategy?		

Question 1 is aimed at establishing one's philosophical approach to teaching cognitive skills. If you answer "yes" to this question, then you are, in effect, a content theorist, and you probably teach mostly by way of the lecture/transmission method. The chances are that you believe that critical thinking must be "infused" into course content and "transmitted" into your students' minds. To the contrary, I reason that subject matter does not require injections of criticality; all subject matter is already critically alive and will naturally take up information to itself, as growing plants absorb nutrients, when allowed to grow analytically.

Question 2 is aimed at getting one to perceive subject matter as more than a sequential series of topics. (For information related to questions 1 and 2, see the discussions of methodology and subject matter in Chapter 3, and the discussion of Means-Ends Critical Analysis of Subject Matter (MECA/SM) that begins with Chapter 5.)

Questions 3 through 10 are aimed at establishing whether the critical-teaching strategy is a conscious one on the part of the teacher, and whether the strategy is operationally shared with students. If you operate in a fully functioning analytical classroom, you can answer "no" to question #1 and "yes" to questions 2 through 10.

Colleagues sometimes tell me that they "already use a form of means-ends strategy" in their classes. If you can answer "yes" to questions 2 through 10, then you probably share my analytical-critical presupposition about subject matter, as queried in questions 1 and 2.

If you are a teacher, you can use the checklist to determine whether your school is largely an analytical school, or the other kind. Do you and you colleagues use means-end analyses? How would your colleagues answer questions 3 through 10?

If you are a school principal, college president, or university administrator, you are probably familiar with the issues raised—or at least the need discussed—in this book. In that case, you also understand the need for a new set of educational principles, a need that can be met with a means-ends approach to critical thinking. Ask yourself the following questions, and act on the answers:

1. When considering a new direction in policy, what impact will this policy, this program, and the expenditure of these funds have on improving the analytical teaching and learning that takes place in the classrooms of my school? How will critical thinking across the curriculum be implemented?

2. How will this policy, this program, and these funds help establish the analytical classroom so that our students may improve their basic, academic, critical, and workplace skills?

If you are a curriculum designer, you are probably aware that assigned learning objectives reinforce the use of the rote-memory, lecture-for-recall, uncritical method. Use the checklist to redesign programs that emphasize analysis, not memorization.

If you are a parent, use the checklist to ask teachers, principals, college and university administrators, and members of local and state boards of education how the financial support that you provide is being used to develop your child's cognitive skills. You will not be satisfied with general answers. Ask to see specific examples of the teaching of cognitive skills within the context of the subject matter being learned in your child's school.

If you are a student, has your teacher taught you to think critically within the context of the subject matter you study? Have your teachers endeavored to bring you and your classmates to conscious awareness of a means-ends

analytical approach to the subject matter that you study?
Do your teachers require a lot of memorization and feed-
back on tests of material memorized from lecture notes
and uncritically accepted from textbooks? Or are your
teachers analytical teachers who emphasize critical analysis of subject matter, who actively engage you in discussing subject matter, who share with you their own
means-ends analytical methods, and who make assignments that require you to exercise and develop your own
cognitive powers?

So, is your school an analytical school?

Bibliography

A Nation at Risk. Washington, D.C.: National Commission on Excellence in Education, 1983.

Action for Excellence. Denver: Education Commission of the United States, 1983.

American Education—Making It Work. Washington, D. C.: United States Department of Education, 1988.

Andre, T. "Does Answering Higher-Level Questions While Reading Facilitate Production of Learning?" *Review of Educational Research 49* (spring, 1979): 280-318.

Armstrong, D. G., J. J. Denton & T. V. Savage, Jr. *Instructional Skills Handbook.* Englewood Cliffs, New Jersey: Educational Technology Publications, 1978.

Astin, A. W. *Achieving Educational Excellence.* San Francisco: Jossey-Bass Publishers, 1985.

Astin, A. W. *Preventing Students from Dropping Out.* San Francisco: Jossey-Bass Publishers, 1975.

Aylesworth, T. G. & G. M. Reagan. *Teaching for Thinking.* Garden City, New York: Doubleday and Company, Inc., 1969.

Black, M. *Critical Thinking,* second edition. New York: Prentice-Hall, 1952.

Bloom, B. S. *et al.*, *Taxonomy of Educational Objectives, Handbook 1: The Cognitive Domain*. New York: Longman, 1956.

Boyer, E. L. *College*. New York: Harper & Row, 1987.

Brookfield, S. D. *Developing Critical Thinkers*. San Francisco: Jossey-Bass Publishers, 1987.

Brown, B. F. *Crisis in Secondary Education*. Englewood Cliffs: Prentice-Hall, 1984.

Bruner, J. S. *Toward a Theory of Instruction*. Cambridge, Massachusetts: Harvard University Press, 1966.

Bruner, J. S. *The Process of Education*. Cambridge, Massachusetts: Harvard University Press, 1977.

Callahan, R. E. *Education and the Cult of Efficiency*. Chicago: The University of Chicago Press, 1962.

Cromwell, L. S. "Critical Thinking: Alverno College Model." Program material for the April 2, 1990 meeting of the American Association for Higher Education—Critical Thinking.

DeCecco, J. P. *The Psychology of Learning and Instruction*. Englewood Cliffs, New Jersey: Prentice-Hall, Inc., 1968.

Defanti, T. A. & M. D. Brown. "Scientific Animation Workstations: Creating an Environment for Remote Research, Education, and Communication," *Academic Computing 3 (February, 1989) : 10-12, 55-57.*

Desowitz, R. S. *The Thorn in the Starfish: The Immune System and How it Works*. New York: W. W. Norton & Company, 1987.

Dewey, J. *Democracy and Education* (copyright 1916 by Macmillan Company) New York: The Free Press, 1966.

Dewey, J. *How We Think*. Boston: D. C. Heath, 1910.

Dewey, J. *How We Think* — A Restatement of the Relation of Reflective Thinking to the Educative Process. Boston: D. C. Heath, 1933.

Dewy, J. *Logic—The Theory of Inquiry.* New York: Henry Holt and Company, 1938.

Eliot, C. W., ed. *The Harvard Classics, American Historical Documents* v. 43. New York: P. F. Collier & Son Company, 1909.

Freire, P. *Education for Critical Consciousness.* New York: The Seabury Press, 1973.

Freire, P. & A. Faundez. *Learning to Question*, New York: Continuum Publishing, 1989.

Furst, E. J. "Bloom's Taxonomy of Educational Objectives for the Cognitive Domain: Philosophical and Educational Issues." *Review of Educational Research 51* (winter, 1981): 441-453.

Gagne, R. M., & L. J. Briggs. *Principles of Instructional Design.* New York: Holt, Rinehart and Winston, Inc., 1974.

Gagne, R. M. & R. T. White. "Memory Structures and Learning Outcomes," *Review of Educational Research 48* (spring, 1978): 187-222.

Greenfield, Lois B. "Teaching Thinking through Problem Solving," in J. E. Stice, ed., *Developing Critical Thinking and Problem Solving Abilities. New Directions for Teaching and Learning, no. 30.* San Francisco, Jossey-Bass Publishers, 1987.

Getzels, J. W. "Creative Thinking, Problem-Solving, and Instruction," in E. R. Hilgard, ed., *Theories of Learning and Instruction*, The Sixty-Third Yearbook of the National Society for the Study of Education. Chicago: The University of Chicago Press (1964): 240-67.

Gordon, I. J., ed. *Criteria for Theories of Instruction.* Washington, D. C.: Association for Supervision and Curriculum Development, NEA, 1968.

Guilford, J. P. *Way beyond the IQ.* Buffalo: The Creative Education Foundation, Inc., 1977.

Haddan, E. E. *Evolving Instruction.* London: Collier-Macmillan Limited, 1970.

Hammerbacher, G. H. "Preparing Faculty to Teach Thinking Skills—The King's College Experience." Program material for the April 2, 1990 meeting of the American Association for Higher Education—Critical Thinking.

Hartman-Hass, H. J. "Improving Cognitive Skills Theory and Practice," *Journal of Developmental and Remedial Education 5* (fall, 1981): 10-30.

Hoeke, M. C. "CAI: A Guideline for Effective Use," *Interface 10* (winter, 1988/1989) : 102-05.

Ingraffea, T. & K. Minks. "Project Socrates," *Academic Computing 3* (October, 1988): 20-21, 60-63.

Involvement in Learning. Washington, D.C.: National Institute of Education, 1984.

Maiorana, Victor P. "The Analytical School and College Classroom." A paper delivered at the annual conference of the Massachusetts Faculty Development Consortium on Improving College Teaching and Learning, Bentley College, Massachusetts, February 14, 1992.

_____. "The Critical Thinking Dimension of John Dewey and Its Impact on Teaching," *Educational Dimensions* (spring, 1985).

_____. *How to Learn and Study in College*. Englewood Cliffs, N.J.: Prentice-Hall Inc., 1980.

_____. "How to Foster Original Work in Writing Assignments," *The Queensborough Review* (fall, 1985).

_____. "An Instructional Design Innovation: Why Not Use Systems Analysis to Teach Systems Analysis?" *The Journal of Computer Information Systems* (fall, 1986).

_____. "Job Skills in the Year 2000, Critical Literacy Strategies, and an Introduction to MECA/SM Methodology." A paper presented at the 1990 New York City Board of Education Business/Finance Cluster Symposium on Workplace Skills and Critical Literacy in the Year 2000 and Beyond. Kennedy Holiday Inn Hotel, March 27, 1990.

_____. *A Model of Teaching Business Management Based on John Dewey's Concept of Critical Thinking,* doctoral dissertation, New York, 1984. Ann Arbor, Michigan: University Microfilm International, 1984.

_____. "The Multicultural Classroom and Purposeful Teaching." A paper delivered at the National Association for Equal Opportunity in Higher Education Conference, Achieving Excellence, Washington, D.C., March 22, 1991.

_____. "Procognitive Individualized Instruction." A paper presented at the 1985 Conference of the Society for Individualized Instruction on Teaching Thinking Skills. Rutgers University, October 11, 1985. [ED 271 094]

_____. "Reinventing the Profession by Teaching Subject Matter and Critical Thinking at the Same Time." Conference proceedings: *Teaching as a Creative Activity,* The International Society for Exploring Teaching Alternatives, Indianapolis, October, 1990, 85-86.

_____. "The Road from Rote to Critical Thinking," *Community Review* (spring, 1992.)

_____. "Teaching Critical Thinking in the Health and Education Curriculum with MECA/SM Methodology." A paper presented at a meeting of the ad-hoc committee on the nursing curriculum, CUNY Office of Academic Affairs, April 20, 1990.

_____. "The University Classroom of the Future: Meeting the Challenge of Change with the Visual Teaching Method." Conference proceedings: *The Future of the University: The Challenge of Change in Europe and America,* University of Perugia, Perugia, Italy (September, 1991): 55-77.

Mason, J. H. *Mathematics Education: Awakening the (Re)Searcher Within*. Milton Keynes, England: Open University, 1991.

Meyers, C. *Teaching Students to Think Critically*. San Francisco: Jossey-Bass Publishers, 1986.

NCRIPTAL. "Faculty Are Traditionalists in Planning Courses," *On Campus 9* (September, 1989): 2.

Nelson-Barber, S. & Meier, T. "Multicultural Context, a Key Factor in Teaching," *Academic Connections, 8* (spring, 1990): 1-5, 9-11.

Osborn, A. F. *Applied Imagination*, third edition. New York: Charles Scribner's Sons, 1963.

Parnes, S. J. "CPSI: The General System," *The Journal of Creative Behavior 2* (March, 1977): 1-11.

Paul R. *Critical Thinking, What Every Person Needs to Survive in a Rapidly Changing World*. Rohnert Park, California: Center for Critical Thinking and Moral Critique, Sonoma State University, 1990.

Paul, R. "Program Material." *Critical Thinking Forum 1989*. Center for Critical Thinking and Moral Critique, Sonoma State University, 1989.

Piaget, J. *Science of Education and the Psychology of the Child*. Middlesex, England: Penguin Books, 1977.

Rorty, R. *Philosophy and the Mirror of Nature*. Princeton: Princeton University Press, 1979.

Rugg, H. *The Teacher of Teachers*, New York: Harper and Brothers, Publishers, 1952.

Schwartz, J. L. "Intellectual Mirrors: A Step in the Direction of Making Schools Knowledge-Making Places," *Harvard Educational Review 59* (February, 1989): 50-61.

Seddon, G. M. "The Properties of Bloom's Taxonomy of Educational Objectives for the Cognitive Domain," *Review of Educational Research 48* (spring, 1978): 303-23.

Seif, E. "Thinking and Education: A Futures Approach," *Journal of Thought 16* (fall, 1981): 73-87.

Semprevivo, P. C. *Systems Analysis: Definition, Process, and Design.* Chicago: Science Research Associates, 1976.

Shermis, S. S. *Critical Thinking: Helping Students Learn Reflectively.* Bloomington, Indiana: ERIC Clearinghouse on Reading and Communication Skills, 1992.

Shor, I. *Critical Teaching in Everyday Life.* Boston: South End Press, 1980.

Siegel, M. & R. F. Carey. *Critical Thinking: A Semiotic Perspective.* Bloomington, Indiana: ERIC Clearinghouse on Reading and Communication Skills; Urbana, Illinois: NCTE, 1989.

Smith, C. B. *A Commitment to Critical Thinking.* New York: Macmillan/McGraw Hill Publishing Co., 1990.

Stice, J. E., ed. *Developing Critical Thinking and Problem-Solving Abilities.* San Francisco: Jossey-Bass Publishers, 1987.

Stoner, J. *Management,* second edition. Englewood Cliffs, New Jersey: Prentice-Hall, 1982.

Stonewater, Jerry K. "Strategies for Problem Solving." in R. E. Young, ed., *Fostering Critical Thinking, New Directions for Teaching and Learning,* no. 3. San Francisco: Jossey-Bass, 1980.

Taba, H. "The Problems in Developing Critical Thinking," *Thinking: The Journal of Philosophy for Children 1* (1959): 3-4.

Taba, H. *Curriculum Development Theory and Practice.* New York: Harcourt, Brace, & World, Inc., 1952.

Taylor, F. W. *Shop Management.* New York: Harper and Brothers Publishers, 1919.

Traub, S. B. "Three MECA/SM Models and Correlation to New York State Syllabus Performance Objectives." A paper presented at the 1990 New York City Board of Education/Finance Cluster Symposium on Workplace Skills and Critical Literacy in the

Year 2000 and Beyond. Kennedy Holiday Inn Hotel, March 27, 1990.

Thomas, J. W. *Varieties of Cognitive Skills: Taxonomies and Models of the Intellect*. Philadelphia: Research for Better Schools, Inc., 1972.

Wellington, D. C. & J. Wellington. *Teaching for Critical Thinking*. New York: McGraw-Hill Book Company, Inc., 1960.

Werthermer, M. "The Syllogism and Productive Thinking," in J. M. Mandler & G. Mandler, eds., *Thinking from Association to Gestalt*. New York: John Wiley and Sons, Inc., 1964.

Whimbey, A. & L. S. Whimbey. *Intelligence Can Be Taught*. New York: E. P. Dutton and Co., Inc., 1975.

Wideman, H. H. & R. D.Owston, "Student Development of an Expert System Case Study," *Journal of Computer-Based Instruction 15* (summer, 1988): 88-94.

Williams, R. E. *The Teaching of Critical Thinking Skills by the Socratic Method in Selected Units of Introduction to Business*. Doctoral dissertation, Utah State University, 1972. Dissertation Abstracts International, 1973, 33, 4818a. University Microfilms No. 73-5617, 101.

Woods, D. R. "How Might I Teach Problem Solving?" in J. E. Stice, ed., *Developing Critical Thinking and Problem Solving Abilities. New Directions for Teaching and Learning, number 30*. San Francisco, Jossey-Bass Publishers, 1987.

Young, R. E., ed. *New Directions for Teaching and Learning, Fostering Critical Thinking*, Number 3. San Francisco: Jossey-Bass Publishers, 1980.

Index